Tinley Park H.S.

FEATURES OF WRITING WITH A PURPOSE

BY JAMES M. MC CRIMMON

Organization

The basic text of Writing with a Purpose is organized into three parts: "Prewriting," "Writing and Rewriting," and "Special Assignments." The prewriting section helps the student plan the whole paper by discovering purpose, generating and using information, stating and outlining a thesis, and mastering patterns of organization. In "Writing and Rewriting" the student learns the uses of various ways of developing paragraphs and sentences, gets experience in making reasonable choices about diction and style, and studies the elements of persuasion, including argument. Each chapter includes exercises in both writing and revising.

The discussion in Parts I and II moves from the whole essay to paragraphs, sentences, and diction. It might have been possible to reverse the direction, beginning with diction and ending with the whole essay. But two major considerations dictate the present order: (1) the decision to begin with prewriting requires a preview of the composition of the whole paper; (2) the present order reflects the actual concerns in freshman composition courses, in which students are asked from the beginning of the course to write complete compositions, not individual sentences.

The longer edition of the text also includes an extensive "Handbook of Grammar and Usage," a "Glossary of Grammatical and Literary Terms," and "A Checklist of Troublesome Usages."

Writing Style

McCrimmon avoids both overly formal and overly colloquial language and addresses his readers in a style that he teaches as one appropriate for most student papers, a moderate style. He is particularly attentive to presenting ideas simply and clearly.

Theoretical Orientation

The author draws freely from the thought and discoveries of contemporary theorists and researchers in rhetoric and language. However, he feels that the major responsibility of the author of a freshman composition textbook is not to report the scholarship in the field but to adapt that scholarship selectively to the needs of students. Consequently, he simplifies complex concepts and expresses them in language that students can understand.

Pedagogy

The inductive method of learning is central to the text's pedagogy. Time after time students are asked to examine details, to discover relationships among the details, and only then to draw conclusions. This methodology is in harmony with the book's theme of purpose.

The basic thesis of the book is that most of the decisions a writer makes at all stages of writing are determined by the answer to two questions: What do I want to say about the subject? How can I best say it for the kind of reader I have in mind? The answer to these two questions is what McCrimmon calls purpose. This emphasis on purpose pervades all of the first three parts of the book.

The emphasis on purpose begins with prewriting, which is the stage in which a writer thinks out a general personal approach to the treatment of the subject. Prewriting is therefore a planning stage. It is McCrimmon's conviction that the more the student plans before beginning to write, the easier the actual writing becomes. Planning directs and controls both the writing and the rewriting, because a writer who has answered the two basic questions of what and how has a standard by which to test the appropriateness of choices that must be made during actual composition. The standard provided by a sense of purpose tends to keep all parts of the composition relevant to the subject and consistent with each other.

Exercises

Writing with a Purpose contains a considerable number of exercises and questions for discussion that are intended to encourage student involvement in the concepts being taught. Some of the exercises are relatively easy, others relatively difficult. Since there are probably more exercises than can be used in many courses, the instructor can choose those that best meet the needs of a particular class.

INSTRUCTOR'S MANUAL

WRITING WITH A PURPOSE

TEACHING WITH A PURPOSE

Webb Salmon
Florida State University

Instructor's Guide and Resource Book for
Writing with a Purpose

Seventh Edition

James M. McCrimmon

Contributing Authors

Susan Miller
The University of Wisconsin--Milwaukee

Webb Salmon
Florida State University

HOUGHTON MIFFLIN COMPANY   BOSTON

Dallas   Geneva, Illinois
Hopewell, New Jersey   Palo Alto   London

Copyright © 1980 by Houghton Mifflin Company. All rights reserved.
Any or all items in this manual may be adapted or reproduced in
any way which will make them more useful or convenient for college
teachers and their classes. Reproduction of these items for com-
mercial purposes is expressly prohibited.

Printed in the U.S.A.

ISBN: 0-395-28254-3

CONTENTS

PREFACE   ix

PART 1   PREWRITING
   1 Purpose: An Overview   3
   2 Getting and Using Information   15
   3 Stating and Outlining a Thesis   25
   4 Common Patterns of Development   35

PART 2   WRITING AND REWRITING
   5 Paragraphs: Units of Development   49
   6 Sentences: Patterns of Expression   64
   7 Diction: The Choice of Words   75
   8 Tone and Style   87
   9 Persuasion   93

PART 3   SPECIAL ASSIGNMENTS
   10 The Essay Examination   111
   11 The Critical Essay: Writing About Literature   117
   13 The Research Paper   135
   14 The Business Letter   143

HANDBOOK OF GRAMMAR AND USAGE   145

BIBLIOGRAPHY   165

PREFACE

The primary intention of <u>Teaching with a Purpose</u> is to provide help for young teachers of composition as they plan how they and their students will use <u>Writing with a Purpose</u>. The intended voice is that of an experienced teacher who has confidence in the pedagogy called for by the text and who has had the opportunity to study the new edition closely during its development.

This instructor's guide contains material about each chapter in <u>Writing with a Purpose</u> except "Using the Library," which is a reference chapter. The guide explains how each chapter in the parts entitled "Prewriting" and "Writing and Rewriting" fits into the organization of the text, and it explains the nature of each chapter in the "Special Assignments" section. When a concept presented in the text is particularly difficult to teach, the guide tries to point a way through the difficulty. It comments on almost all of the exercises, and when one of them requires more preparation time than a busy teacher is likely to have, it presents part of the preparation. The guide gives answers to the exercises in the "Handbook of Grammar and Usage" (in the full edition of the text), and it contains an annotated bibliography of books and articles relevant to the teaching of composition.

For help in the preparation of <u>Teaching with a Purpose</u>, I am indebted to James McCrimmon. He wrote critiques of the manuscript and conferred with me about it, and in some instances he drafted copy for me to consider. A teacher cannot expect to have many opportunities to work with such a colleague.

My other major indebtedness is to my wife, Joyce, who did so much to get the manuscript ready for the publisher.

Webb Salmon

INSTRUCTOR'S MANUAL

WRITING WITH A PURPOSE

PART 1

PREWRITING

CHAPTER 1   PURPOSE: AN OVERVIEW

Writing with a Purpose emphasizes the importance of the writer's thinking. This emphasis grows out of Professor McCrimmon's belief that good writing is usually the product of a process that can be taught to almost all students who are able and willing to think carefully about the process. The book almost says, "If students can think purposefully about their writing, they can write well, or at least better."

For a number of years composition teachers have associated Writing with a Purpose with the importance of prewriting, the stage in which the student does much of his or her thinking about the writing. This stage is so important in the writing process that the first four chapters of the text treat prewriting. But McCrimmon encourages students to continue to think critically about their essays on through the writing and rewriting stages.

Writing with a Purpose begins, appropriately, with a chapter on purpose. In previous editions McCrimmon has begun the chapter with a definition of purpose. In this edition he has decided that purpose is such a complex term that students will understand it better if he leads up to it through a discussion of its chief components: situation, reader, and real subject. This inductive approach leads into the section called "Your View of Your Purpose," in which purpose is defined and students are asked to examine in detail a paper that illustrates the effects of a freshman writer's knowing what he wanted to do and how he wanted to do it--that is, the effects of the young writer's knowing and carrying out his purpose. The quality of this paper, which concludes the chapter, is an excellent illustration of what Professor McCrimmon means when he says in the first sentence of this first chapter, "Writing is, first of all, a way of thinking, and the quality of your writing will depend to a large extent on the quality of the thinking you do about your subject both before and during the writing."

Questions for Discussion (page 5)

1. Allen says that once he has settled on a subject he begins gathering information. In the prewriting stage he takes notes as he selects from material that he happens upon ("a good line" that he hears) and as he does research into his subject. Allen begins the writing stage only after he has done a good deal of thinking about his subject. In the writing stage, he lets the

material "take shape" as he writes. In the rough draft he concentrates on making his purpose clear and holding his reader's interest. Then he writes a second draft, concentrating at this stage on improving his ideas and perfecting his language. After some time has elapsed, Allen checks the structure of his writing, reshaping if necessary. Sometimes he finds that he has strayed from his purpose; in that event he throws his writing away and begins anew.

2. Allen emphasizes what he does before and after he writes his rough draft. He stresses, then, the prewriting and rewriting stages of his work.

3. As your students compare their writing procedures with Allen's, some may say that their prewriting is similar to his; others may confess that they begin writing without having done much information gathering and thinking about the subject; and a few may point out that, unlike Allen, they try to shape their papers by outlining before they begin writing. Few if any of your students will say that they concentrate on rewriting as much as Allen does.

4. Allen's acknowledgment, "I don't really know everything I think about something until I put it on paper," is in harmony with McCrimmon's statement that "the actual writing clarifies your ideas." Other writers have had this experience that Allen describes: ". . . Often I find what I write is a trigger toward something bigger that I didn't realize I knew." Robert Frost speaks of a similar revelation he sometimes experienced while writing poetry: "For me the initial delight is in the surprise of remembering something I didn't know I knew." ("The Figure a Poem Makes")

5. Perhaps the two most helpful points that your students can learn from the interview are these: (a) the writer should not begin to write before thinking carefully about the subject and before gathering and sorting material; (b) the writer should be willing to examine drafts impersonally and critically and to rewrite until the essay is as good as he or she can make it.

A precautionary note is in order. As McCrimmon explains (page 5), student writers are not likely to be so competent as professionals in discovering what needs to be changed in an early draft. Furthermore, the pressure of time often limits the amount of rewriting students can do. Therefore Allen's practice of letting the material take its shape in the rough draft may not serve students well, particularly when they are writing long papers. The text will advocate careful prewriting that to a considerable extent shapes the essay before the writing stage begins.

YOUR VIEW OF THE WRITING SITUATION

A fundamental question for a writer to consider is this: "Who is speaking to whom, on what subject, and in what situation?" Your students may have thought little in the past about how the

Purpose: An Overview   5

situation determines what a writer may appropriately say. You can help them begin to understand this element of writing by setting up problem situations and asking their judgment about the influence the situations should have on the writing of the persons involved. Here are three example situations; you may want to create others that you know will be meaningful to your students.

Situation 1

An undergraduate has written a paper for presentation before his speech class denouncing the existence in our military forces of elitist troops such as the Green Berets. His speech emphasizes the appeal he believes such forces have for militaristic minds and argues that their existence seems to legitimize the commission of atrocities (such as the summary execution of captured spies) during wartime. Two days before he is to deliver his speech, he learns from a classmate that a young woman in the class had an older brother who was a member of the Green Berets in Vietnam until he was captured and executed by the enemy. How will the new element in the situation influence what the speaker will say?

a. Should he give the speech he has prepared?

b. Should he revise the speech, denouncing the sort of emotional appeal that does young men a disservice by luring them into elitist forces?

c. Should he revise the speech, giving the history of elitist forces in the military but offering no opinion about whether the forces should exist?

d. Should he make some other decision?

Situation 2

A number of years ago a minor federal government official agreed to make a speech to an audience some distance from Washington. As was the custom in his office, he ran off half a dozen copies of his speech a week before it was due and passed them around to his colleagues for suggestions and criticisms. A week later, he checked into a hotel the night before he was to speak, got a good night's sleep, and went down to breakfast the next morning. On the way into the dining room, he bought a newspaper and found his speech printed as one made by the President the night before. Evidently one of the copies he had passed out had been referred to the President. What should the speaker have done?

a. Explain goodnaturedly that the speech must have been mistaken for one written by the President's writers, and go ahead and give the speech as he wrote it?

b. Complain that the President had given his speech?

6   Teaching with a Purpose

c. Abandon his prepared speech and speak extemporaneously on a related subject?

d. Take some other approach?

Situation 3

The new governor campaigned on a "law-and-order" platform, stressing among other matters that (1) he believes capital punishment to be moral, even after listening carefully to many arguments to the contrary, and (2) his review of many studies has convinced him that the death penalty may be a deterrent to murder. Now the governor is faced with the decision of whether to sign the execution order for a person who has been convicted of first-degree murder and whose lawyers have unsuccessfully exhausted all the legal appeals available to the convicted man. No execution has occurred in the state for many years. But a reliable survey shows that more than two-thirds of the adults in the state favor the death penalty for first-degree murder.

A citizen who is opposed to the death penalty for what she considers to be both moral and practical reasons will write to the governor, trying to persuade him not to sign the execution order. What approach does the situation suggest that she should take?

a. Should she argue that the death penalty is immoral?

b. Should she argue that the death penalty is not a deterring force against murder?

c. Should she explain that she believes an execution will cause future jurors, who will not want to bear responsibility for taking a person's life, to convict first-degree murderers of second-degree murder? She is concerned that these criminals could be paroled after a few years and return to society to kill again.

d. Should she tell the governor that if he signs the execution order she will work to mobilize public opinion against him?

e. Is there some other argument that she might make--or some combination of arguments?

YOUR VIEW OF YOUR READER

As McCrimmon points out, the travel directions on page 7 do not call for the kind of reader analysis that some class papers will, particularly papers in persuasion. But the directions do show that even in such elementary discourse, what the speaker says is influenced by what he knows about the person he is addressing. To illustrate this point, you can ask your students to rewrite the directions, assuming that instead of speaking to a person who is unfamiliar with the city, the speaker is addressing someone who knows the city well and simply needs to know the easiest route from

the Holiday Inn to the speaker's house. The directions might go
like this:

> Drive east on Main to Magnolia. Turn right onto
> Magnolia and go to U.S. 27. Continue across 27 to
> Pine. Turn left onto Pine. The fifth driveway on
> the left is mine.

The person addressed here does not need the information that would
help a stranger anticipate the reference points, and so what the
speaker tells her is quite different from what he says to the
person who does not know the city.

You may want to emphasize this point about the writer's view
of the reader by asking your students to write two sets of directions intended to move a person from one point to another in your
town or city. One set should be for a stranger, the other for a
person familiar with the locality. By reading or hearing each
other's papers, students can offer advice about whether the speaker
has been clear in each set of directions.

Exercise A (pages 8-9)

The Marco Beach Hotel & Villas advertisement is intended to
appeal to active, gregarious people. Even though the island is
"very tropical" and "very secluded" and even though sandpipers
call, the emphasis is on walking the beach, playing golf and
tennis, and enjoying nighttime parties filled with music and
laughter. The picture of the friendly young couple and the large
hotel assures the reader that lots of other people will be there.
On the other hand, the Peter Island advertisement is intended to
appeal to affluent people who patronize "very good travel agents"
and want to spend their money in a quiet environment free of
"every Tom, Dick, and Harry." Even though the ad admits that "you
can sail, snorkel, and ride" and "you can fish, canoe, play tennis,
and scuba dive," the emphasis is on thinking, enjoying "peace and
solitude," and doing "nothing at all." The picture of the solitary
young woman, water, and an uninhabited island suggests that one can
vacation in privacy.

The exercise instructions suggest that the two resorts may be
quite similar but that these advertisements are designed to appeal
to particular readers. To emphasize this point, you can tell your
students that another Marco Beach Hotel & Villas ad pictures a
young family, advertises the resort as "a kid's paradise" with
"free children's programs," and says nothing about the night life--
and that another advertisement of Peter's Island, obviously written
to appeal to readers other than those who would be attracted by the
ad shown in the text, says nothing about the expensiveness of the
resort and nothing about the absence of "every Tom, Dick, and
Harry."

8   Teaching with a Purpose

Exercise B (page 9)

The advertisements that your students write will differ greatly, of course, because of the students' varying interests, past experiences on vacations, and imaginations. But a brief examination of resort advertisements intended to attract college age students suggests that the ads are likely to emphasize the outdoors, vigorous and even adventurous physical activity, travel to distant places, and good food. Your students may decide that their ads should either say or imply that the resort is affordable for people with limited funds.

Whatever the content of a good ad, it should address such concerns as these: What makes an ideal setting for college students on vacation? What do they want to do while they are there? Can people on typical student budgets afford the resort, or do the owners intend to attract only those young people with lucrative part-time employment or generous parents?

YOUR VIEW OF YOUR SUBJECT

GENERAL AND "REAL" SUBJECTS

Teachers often complain that students move from one generalization to another in their papers, leaving out supporting details. Students are likely to respond that they must resort to this method of writing if they are to discuss their subjects within the space limitations specified by the instructor or in the amount of time allocated for an in-class paper. Sometimes the problem is that they are trying to write on a general subject rather than on what McCrimmon calls a real subject. You should be able to appeal to your students' self-interest by explaining that learning to write on real subjects can help solve their space and time problems.

You will find it necessary to talk closely with your students about the concept of "real subject," even though they have read about it. They need to know that both restriction and focus distinguish a real from a general subject. These two characteristics are related, of course: the restriction of a broad subject makes it possible for the writer to focus on the central idea that controls the paper. A real subject differs from a restricted one in that the real subject suggests what the paper will say about the subject.

To help your students understand the concepts discussed here, you can conduct a discussion session in which they will practice moving from general through restricted subjects to real subjects. The two diagrams that follow can serve as models. Once the students see how the restricting and focusing process works, they can create other examples with your guidance. Board work will be essential here, of course: you or the recording student can write suggestions, erase false starts, and write in the improved recommendations until the class has arrived at manageable real subjects.

Purpose: An Overview 9

General subject	Rights of students
Restricted subject	Visiting regulations in dorms / Grade-appeal systems
Real subject	Positive and negative effects of an experiment in permissive visiting regulations in dorms / The unfairness of the grade-appeal system in our college

General subject	Problems caused by smoking
Restricted subject	Health problems caused by smoking / Nonsmokers' objections to smoking
Real subject	Correlation of rising rate of lung cancer in women with increased smoking by women / Results of a survey of what nonsmokers find objectionable about smoking

General subject	Balance of power in the U.S. system of government
Restricted subject	Powers shared between the executive and the legislative branches / State power vs. federal power in educational issues
Real subject	How the President and the Senate bargained on the lifting of trade restrictions on Rhodesia / Why federal regulations can influence policymaking in state-owned universities

Questions for Discussion (page 13)

The questions in this discussion exercise are sufficiently detailed and structured for the students to discover what prevents "On Your Own" from being a satisfactory paper. The basic problem, of course, is that the essay, from the second paragraph on, does not discuss the subject that the title and first paragraph suggest it will. Indeed, instead of being on his own, the student seems to have had help at just about every turn.

Another and related problem is that the writer does not always develop the idea with which a paragraph begins. In paragraph two he begins by talking about how busy he was during Freshman Week but goes on to say how much he enjoyed meeting his dorm mates. In the third paragraph he starts again to speak of his busy schedule, but by the fourth sentence he is explaining how he got his schedule approved. These paragraphs may surprise the reader, following as they do the carefully disciplined opening paragraph. The last two paragraphs are inferior to the first, but they are improvements over the second and third paragraphs. (Problems in paragraph

10   Teaching with a Purpose

development like those existing in "On Your Own" will be discussed in detail in Chapter 5, but you may find it advisable to discuss them briefly at this point.)

Your students may feel that the writer just quit, rather than concluding his essay. Perhaps by the time he reached the end, he thought he was writing about the help that the students gave each other. If that were his subject, the abruptness of the ending would be less conspicuous. But neither the idea of mutual help nor any other idea pervades the essay. The student needs to decide what his real subject is and then start over with his writing.

Your students can profitably compare the lack of control obvious in "On Your Own" with the admirable control that marks "Is Dating Outdated?" and "The Roles I Play." Invite them to find evidence in these last two essays that either of the writers was unaware of her purpose or that she departed from her real subject. It will be difficult to find such evidence.

YOUR VIEW OF YOUR PURPOSE

Now that McCrimmon has discussed the writer's view of (a) the writing situation, (b) the reader, and (c) the subject, he is ready to say explicitly what <u>purpose</u>, as used in the text, means: "the basic commitments writers make when determining (1) what they want to do, and (2) how they want to do it." As he points out, purpose is concerned with both the what and the how of a paper--with both content and style.

This perception of purpose will require explanation from you, for it is both basic to what the text teaches and different from your students' understanding of the word <u>purpose</u>. Their meaning may permit them to say, "My purpose is to advocate reforms in our penal system" or "My purpose is to explain what an ideal education should be," without considering what the writing situation is, what influence the nature of the audience will have on what is said and how it is said, and how the subject can be restricted and brought into sharp focus. The concept of purpose that McCrimmon advocates is not learned suddenly. But students will come to understand its value to the writer as you insist in paper after paper that they need to know what they want to do and how they want to do it.

The two paragraphs (page 17) that introduce "Why We Need More Westerns on Television" give a good explanation of how a writer can proceed from (1) deciding on a general subject to (2) narrowing it to a restricted subject to (3) determining the real subject to (4) discovering her purpose. You can emphasize these paragraphs profitably when the class discusses this student essay.

Questions for Discussion (pages 18-19)

1. The author's satire of Americans' fascination with westerns on television is evident from the beginning to the ending of the essay. We are likely to assume, then, that she knew her purpose

from the time she began writing. Her control of the writing is admirable, especially since few students can keep an ironic paper from getting out of hand. The tendency is for the irony to become too heavy, to lose its subtlety. (Some students may think that this tendency shows occasionally in the paper. The last sentence of the second paragraph could have been deleted; the last clause of the third paragraph approaches sarcasm instead of remaining irony; in the fourth paragraph everything from <u>fair and square</u> to the end is a bit too heavy. But these defects are only minor flaws in an unusually fine student paper.)

2. The structure of the essay is simple and effective. The first paragraph announces the (pretended) thesis--we need more westerns on television--and ends with a commitment: "I'll tell you what I mean." In the next three paragraphs the writer does just that, making a point in each paragraph to support her thesis: westerns teach us to make friends (paragraph 2), they teach us "the difference between good people and bad people" (paragraph 3), and they teach us "our country's history" (paragraph 4). The last paragraph restates the thesis in the first sentence: ". . . we ought to have more of them."

Sometimes students wonder whether a last paragraph that refers back to the first must be almost identical with the first. You can ask your students whether the first and last paragraphs in this paper are interchangeable. The answer, of course, is no--one introduces and the other sums up. If their positions were reversed, they would not work nearly so well as they do.

This five-paragraph paper can serve you well if you are concerned with trying to modify the practice that so many students have developed by the time they take a freshman composition course: stating in the first paragraph the three points the paper will make, developing in the next three paragraphs the three points the opening paragraph promised, and restating in the last paragraph the three points that have just been developed. There is no such monotony in "Why We Need More Westerns on Television," though it is indeed a five-paragraph paper with an introduction; three paragraphs, each of which makes a point that supports the thesis; and a concluding paragraph.

3. Different readers will discover the spoof at different points in the essay. Most may see it by the time they read the phrase "early enough for the kids to see it" (line 6). If they do not recognize it there, then they certainly will have done so by the time they have read the last sentence in the first paragraph. As they look back over the essay they will see, of course, that the spoof begins in the very first sentence with <u>wonderful</u>.

4. Someone determined to hold the writer responsible for the effectiveness of the illustrations might point out that the reader cannot be certain whether the second paragraph is speaking

primarily of personal friendship or of international peace. But that reader would be missing part of the fun that the writer has when she, with tongue in cheek, forces the two concepts together. And a reader might object to the last paragraph, observing that (1) Indians are often portrayed in westerns as primarily noble rather than primarily pagan and (2) the portrayal of the Indians is only one of a number of different ways in which television westerns distort the history of the country (notorious outlaws were really fine fellows who got a bad break, conflicts between Yankees and Rebs were ideological in ways not related to political machinations occurring in the more settled areas of the country, railroad executives were primarily concerned about opening up the West so the nation could achieve its "manifest destiny" and never intended to defraud farmers by charging ruinous freight rates). But the writer makes no pretense of presenting a complete case against westerns and should not be held responsible for making one.

5. If the paper were a straightforward, entirely serious denunciation of television westerns, the language that borders on colloquialism would not be appropriate. But though the paper makes a serious point through irony, its tone of necessity is light. So there should be no objection to the very informal language.

6. The statement about what Americans are not interested in is appropriate, for the essay is a satire on Americans' taste in television shows, not just a satire on the shows themselves.

7. The predominant attitude will probably be that the writer planned for her readers to join her in the fun--and had confidence that they would. A critic who thinks the occasional lack of subtlety in the essay shows that the writer does not trust her readers may not be aware of how rare it is for a writer to sustain the subtlety typical of the best irony.

8. If the speaker is the author, then what has been said about the irony in the piece is wrong and the author is a naive young woman who writes well. But there should be no real doubt that the speaker is a narrator deliberately created by an author very much aware of her purpose.

This paper is a good illustration of what McCrimmon means when he states the dominant idea advocated by <u>Writing with a Purpose</u> that "the effectiveness of your writing will depend on the clearness with which you see your purpose" (page 19).

Review Exercise A (pages 20-23)

1. The subject is appropriate: it discusses a significant issue, and it is interesting to students. If some students disagree with the thesis, such disagreement does not mean that the essay is inappropriate for them.

Purpose: An Overview 13

2. Your students may disagree about whether the writer had his audience clearly in mind. One indication that he did is his explanation of the legal bounds of "stop-and-frisk" procedure; he knew that his audience would not be knowledgeable about these bounds. He knew that some class members would object to his thesis (he and his instructor discussed this matter when he was planning his paper), and he tried to speak to those objections by presenting the citizen's point of view and speaking of citizens' rights in his last four paragraphs.

3. The three points of view are those of (a) the involved citizen, (b) the involved officer, and (c) the relatively detached writer. The third view contains elements of both the first and second views.

4. The three parts of the essay are (a) a statement of the officer's case, (b) a statement of the citizen's case, and (c) the writer's explanation of the responsibilities and rights of both the officer and the citizen. Each unit is a partial fulfillment of the commitment made in the title.

5. The structure of the essay is too unusual for it to be the result of happenstance. It is obvious that the writer planned to present two different and involved views of the incident before synthesizing them in a detached view in which he would state his thesis. Even those students who disagree with the writer will acknowledge that he recognized that his thesis, "Citizens should willingly cooperate with police officers involved in 'stop-and-frisk' work," is controversial and that he tried to work out his strategy accordingly.

6. Students will differ about whether the plan for the paper is an effective one. Those who will not listen to the argument because their minds are already made up or those who do listen but find the argument unconvincing may reject the plan.

7. Your students may find the information clearer and more complete than did some of the writer's classmates. Your students will be able to study the printed essay before they respond; the writer's classmates responded immediately to an oral presentation. Some apparently responded to what they thought he would say rather than to what he actually did say. Perhaps they were sufficiently out of sympathy with the policeman that they did not hear the last four paragraphs accurately. (The failure of some students to listen with open minds was understandable: grave mistakes made by a few seemingly irresponsible narcotics agents were getting national attention at the time.)

8. The student told his instructor that he had grown up hearing the conversation of narcotics agents who were in his home. Undoubtedly he received some of his information from his father, whom he respected as a very competent agent. And since his father was a full-time, long-term agent, printed material on "stop-and-frisk" laws was almost certainly readily available to the writer.

9. A good way to generate discussion about this paper is to ask your students to study the essay carefully and decide whether it is an excellent, good, average, or unsatisfactory essay. Have them jot down their evaluations so that their decisions will be firm before you begin to record their decisions on the board. Ask two or three of them who rated the paper "excellent" (or considered that rating, if no one actually awarded it) to speak very briefly about what is admirable about the paper and to say nothing about its faults. Then ask two or three who rated the paper "unsatisfactory" (or who assigned the lowest rating, if no one rated it as unsatisfactory) to speak briefly about its weaknesses and to say nothing about its strengths. Explain that no one else (including you) will be allowed to speak until these short speeches are finished and that then anyone who can get the floor may speak. You will have to decide, of course, how much you should say in the last part of the discussion.

CHAPTER 2   GETTING AND USING INFORMATION

Chapter 1 emphasizes the importance of disciplined thinking as the writer discovers the purpose that will control his or her writing. Chapter 2 capitalizes on what has been said about purpose as it discusses four sources of information and then presents a method for interpreting information. The chapter is concerned primarily with teaching the student to move from the discovery of information to the use of the information in a paper.

SOURCES OF INFORMATION

The four sources of information considered in the chapter are these:

   Selecting information from experience

   Observing the subject

   Asking questions about the subject

   Making inferences from the facts

SELECTING INFORMATION FROM EXPERIENCE

This section encourages students to use what they already know in prewriting a paper. McCrimmon is not recommending that students simply write some unrelated bits of information they have, nor is he suggesting that they write straight autobiographical statements. Instead, he is encouraging students to see relationships among different pieces of information or different experiences in their memories and to assimilate this information as they focus their thinking on a real subject. The discussion questions in this section show the effects of such assimilation, and the exercise requires it.

Questions for Discussion (page 27)

1. If the illustrations are left out of the passage about blame, it reads like this:

16   Teaching with a Purpose

> [The refusal to accept responsibility for fault] expresses the deep conviction of multitudes of irresponsibles in the age of self-pity. It is a curious paradox that, while the self is the center of all things, the self is never to blame for anything.
> The fault is always the fault of someone or something else.
> Blame it on God, the girls, or the government, on heredity, or on the environment, on the parents, on the siblings, on the cold war, on the pressures toward conformity, on being unloved and unwanted. But don't blame it on me, the very center around which the universe revolves.

The writer still announces his point, but the reader gets little more than an undeveloped announcement.

2. Appropriate illustrations clarify a generalization by saying in effect, "Here is what I mean." By showing that specifics support the generalization, the illustrations make the point more convincing than it would be without examples.

3. Item *a* is irrelevant to the basic point of the passage. It would not be appropriate.
Item *b* supports the point. It would be appropriate.
Item *c* supports the point. Appropriate.
Item *d* contradicts the point. Not appropriate, unless the subject of the discussion is to be expanded.

Exercise (page 28)

Encourage your students to jot down more than just two or three illustrations so they can select two that will work together harmoniously in a unified statement.

Suppose a student jots down these six regrets.

1. The time on Interstate 10 when I did not stop to help an elderly woman whose automobile tire was flat

2. The day I heard Bob's parents were separating and I said nothing to him

3. My refusal to be a candidate for senior class president when I was nominated

4. My inability to speak to Jane just after she had learned that her mother was dead

5. My decision not to play football my senior year

6. The time I did not accept a summer job back-packing supplies to a Green Mountain hostelry

Getting and Using Information   17

Had he stopped listing illustrations after the first two or three, he probably would have written two paragraphs that had little in common. But 2 and 4 or 3 and 5 should work together in a unified statement, just like the three illustrations in the model paragraph about refusal to accept responsibility.

OBSERVING THE SUBJECT

In this section McCrimmon acknowledges that the "looking at" stage often precedes the "looking for" stage. But he stresses that the kind of looking most helpful to the writer is the disciplined observation that occurs when one is looking for significant details and relationships between details.

The material that follows McCrimmon's comments about observation provides the student with, first, a description of meaningful observation and, second, an exercise that requires the student to observe. The Agassiz piece is an account of a student learning to proceed from looking at to the stage of looking for significant details. The exercise based on Edith, Christmas A.M. asks the students to do their own observing and to arrange their observations into an overall description of the room.

Questions for Discussion (page 31)

1. Agassiz insists that from the beginning of the student's training as a scientist he must learn to rely on close observation and thinking about what he has observed.

2. At the time he was beginning his training, the student was not enthusiastic about the method of instruction. Later he decided that this first lesson was "the best entomological lesson I ever had." We are not told specifically why the lesson was a good one; the student would realize later, of course, that observing details and then reflecting on their interrelationship is the basic approach of a scientist for arriving at conclusions.

3. At the beginning the student did not know what or how to look for, so he just looked at the fish.

4. In order to draw an object accurately, one has to observe its details closely. The drawing, then, requires close observation.

5. Agassiz probably realized that the student was about to see the importance of the parts he was observing to the fish's living and maneuvering. He was almost ready to draw conclusions based on relationships among the details he had been observing.

6. The looking at stage preceded the night of reflection. Because of his thinking about what he had been seeing and the professor's explanation next morning of the significance of a particular observation ("the symmetrical sides with paired organs"), the student was ready to begin the stage of looking for. Now

he was ready to begin to see a pattern in his observations and to look _for_ additional evidence of that pattern.

Exercise (pages 31, 32)

Since different students will attach significance to different details, their lists may be quite dissimilar. The first five observations below reflect the viewer's fascination with the disarray of the room. The last two show the viewer's interest in the age of the room and its furnishings and decorations.

--Gift-wrapping paper covers the floor. It must be cleaned up. Wrapping the packages required so much time, and they looked so pretty an hour ago.

--Christmas gifts, which a little while ago were around the tree, now lie all over the room. They must be put away.

--The various Christmas decorations must be stored until next year.

--The clothes that Edith's husband received for Christmas are lying across a chair.

--The little boy is unconcerned about the mess. He is interested only in playing with his Christmas toys.

--There is much evidence that the house is an old one: the high ceiling, the walls and ceiling made of tongue and groove boards, the electric cord and bulb hanging from the center of the ceiling, the fireplace once used for heating but now enclosed, the mantel around and over the fireplace.

--Some of the decorations and furnishings in the room are old and some are modern: the paper bells and the mirror are clearly old-fashioned; the reclining chair is clearly modern. Other items are harder to date: the wreaths, the lamps.

ASKING QUESTIONS ABOUT THE SUBJECT

After your students have read the piece concerning the questions about the water glass and before they begin the writing assignment called for in the exercise on page 33, they would profit from a question-asking session over which you preside. Your purpose, which you will explain to them, will be to show the students that their questions about a subject will be most helpful if they structure them to show relationships between different parts of the subject.

As a basis for the question session, choose a current issue that most students will know something about and at least a few are likely to be well informed about. Here are some possibilities: a disagreement between student government officials and your college's administrators, controversial charges by the college newspaper against someone or some group, a controversy between a well-known professional athlete and his administrative superiors, a charge of dishonesty or incompetence in state or national government.

You might ask your students to respond to such questions as these: What is the basic stance of A in this controversy? Of B? What are the main differences between their positions? On what do they agree? Is there a history of controversy between A and B? If so, what has been its nature? What do you know about A and B that will help you to form an opinion about their trustworthiness in this particular controversy? Do you know who is likely to support or oppose A and B? Why? What is your best judgment about the outcome of the controversy? In the discussion you will need to be alert to capitalize on questions and answers that are helping the class to discover what they want to know about the issue. And you will want to abandon parts of the discussion that are irrelevant to the issue or otherwise obviously nonproductive.

MAKING INFERENCES FROM THE FACTS

Be sure your students understand the thought process of making an inference, not only because inferences are sources of information but also because they will need to know about inferences later in the course, especially when they study the chapter on persuasion.

Exercise (pages 34-35)

In these answers the second stage is called an assumption. For each inference the student has to provide the assumption. In two items (6 and 10) the student will have to expand the inference to identify all three stages.

1. a. This is a green apple. (observation)
   b. Green apples taste sour. (assumption)
   c. This apple will be sour. (conclusion)

2. a. That cloud is black. (observation)
   b. Rain develops from a black cloud. (assumption)
   c. It is going to rain. (conclusion)

3. a. The faucet keeps dripping. (observation)
   b. A faulty washer causes a faucet to drip. (assumption)
   c. The faucet needs a new washer. (conclusion)

4. a. My car is missing from the parking lot. (observation)
   b. Cars are often stolen from parking lots. (assumption)
   c. My car has been stolen. (conclusion)

5. a. I answered only three of the five questions on the test. (observation)
   b. Sixty percent is not a passing grade. (assumption)
   c. I probably failed. (conclusion)

6. a. She has certain clearly identifiable symptoms. (observation)

b. Those symptoms are often a sign of appendicitis. (assumption)
   c. Her symptoms point to appendicitis. (conclusion)

7. a. It is the third accident at that intersection this month. (observation)
   b. Traffic lights help to prevent accidents. (assumption)
   c. The city should install a traffic light. (conclusion)

8. a. There's plenty of gas in the car. (observation)
   b. Worn spark plugs and the absence of gas are two reasons for a car's not starting. (assumption)
   c. Maybe I need to replace the spark plugs. (conclusion)

9. a. She has not done any of the assignments. (observation)
   b. Anyone who does not do the assignments is sure to fail. (assumption)
   c. She is sure to fail. (conclusion)

10. a. The sky is red tonight. (observation)
    b. A red sky at night often precedes a calm sea. (assumption)
    c. The sailors look forward to a calm sea. (conclusion)

    a. The sky is red this morning. (observation)
    b. A red sky in the morning often precedes a rough sea. (assumption)
    c. The sailors fear that they will experience a rough sea. (conclusion)

INTERPRETING INFORMATION

The method presented in Chapter 2 for interpreting information is basic to much of the thinking about writing that the students will do. It is essential that they learn the method early and understand that they will be able to use it time after time in the course.

Your students need to understand that valid interpretation grows out of close observation of their material. Much bad writing comes from leaping to a conclusion and then rigging the details of the evidence (observations) to support the conclusion. Such rigging is particularly reprehensible because it leads the writer into superficial and erroneous judgments. This chapter advocates the inductive method of arriving at conclusions and explains the steps for using it.

The inductive method has three steps: (1) observing details, (2) seeing relationships among the details, and (3) drawing conclusions based on these relationships. These steps are useful in thinking about any situation in which interpretation is necessary, including argument and critical writing. Because this method provides a simple and logical procedure for arriving at conclusions about a subject, it can be exceptionally valuable for students. It can help them discover the thesis or conclusion to be developed, and it will provide the information needed for developing it.

Getting and Using Information   21

Because the steps are simple and logical, most of your students can learn the method quickly. But they may see it as a method usable only in their immediate writing situations. You will, then, need to stress its general applicability to writing, indeed to much of their work in college.

Exercises (pages 36-40)

The material that follows should be useful as you help your students prepare to write about the Hogarth prints. First, there are observations about the second picture similar to those your students are likely to write. Material in parentheses gives information that the students will not have because (1) the details can be observed only if one has a larger picture than that in the text, or (2) information not explicitly provided in the pictures is necessary to make certain observations. You will probably want to give your students the information that a larger copy of the picture would provide, but you should refrain from telling them anything that suggests interpretation until you come to the interpretive stage. Following the observations are some interpretations and a conclusion about the picture. Finally, there is some additional information that you may find helpful if you want to discuss the Hogarth prints thoroughly. If you do present information that goes beyond what is observable in the pictures, take care that you do not stray from your basic purpose--to teach your students how to use observation and logical thinking as they discover what to say about a subject.

OBSERVATIONS

1. The man in the right foreground is pausing to drink a mug of beer. He seems to be in charge of the books packed into the basket and secured with a rope. (The books are almost certainly some that Hogarth disapproved of.) According to the label on the basket, they are destined for the trunk maker. Pages from books that went unsold were often used in trunk linings. The labels on the books are Lauder on Milton, Modern Tragedies Vol. 12, Hill on Royal Societies, Turnbull on Ancient Painting, and Politicks Vol. 9999. (See the Paulson, Ireland, and Shesgreen works cited on page 23 in this guide.)

2. To the left of the books two fishwives are reading (perhaps singing) the words of a manuscript one holds. (The title of the manuscript is "A New Ballad on the Herring Fishery"; the author is a Mr. Lockman.) The fish baskets are full. One of the women has a mug of beer.

3. To their left a drayman, whispering into the ear of an attractive maid, is holding a mug of beer in one hand, touching the maid's dress at her bosom with the other. She holds a key. Beside her is a basket of food, probably vegetables.

4. To their left are two tradesmen with overflowing beer mugs. One of them (a blacksmith) holds a hindquarter of meat (mutton)

aloft. On the table beside the other are several pages on which there is writing. (One of the written items is a newspaper, The Daily Advertiser. The other is a copy of the king's speech to Parliament. The visible section of the speech reads, "Let me earnestly recommend to you the Advancement of Our Commerce and cultivating the Arts of Peace, in which you may depend on My hearty Concurrence and Encouragement.")

5. Above the tradesmen an artist, the only person in the picture who is poorly clothed, is using a (gin) bottle as a model for an advertisement. Another advertisement showing well-clothed dancers around and on a grain stack (the caption reads "Health to the Barley Mow") stands above the picture the artist is painting. (Perhaps Hogarth wanted to observe that the artist did not share in the nation's prosperity. But more significance may lie in the fact that the impoverished artist--a burlesque of a Hogarth contemporary?--is using a gin bottle--his own?--as a model for the advertisement.)

6. Opposite the artist, the pawnbroker's building stands in disrepair. He reaches through an opening in his door for a small mug of beer (all he can afford?). (The pawnbroker's cat lies dead at his door. His symbol, the mousetrap, is visible through his window.)

7. In the right center background the men who have been carrying a person in a sedan chair pause to drink a beer.

8. In the far background artisans work on the roof of a well-kept building. The building is probably a brewery, for a large beer keg is being lowered from or raised to the upper floor.

INTERPRETATION

1. Most of the people portrayed here seem happy and prosperous. The place is active with trade and labor. Most of the buildings are in good repair.

2. There seems to be some association between the people's contented lives and their enjoyment of drinking beer with their friends.

3. The exceptional people in the picture are the artist and the pawnbroker. Significantly, the artist, apparently a very poor man, is painting an advertisement for gin. The pawnbroker is denied the pleasure of the company of the other people. His building is in ill repair, probably because he has no business in this prosperous place.

CONCLUSION

The "real" subject of this picture is the prosperity and happiness that pervades a place where the people drink beer to the

Getting and Using Information   23

exclusion of the gin that the artist is advertising. (Hogarth's name for the picture is "Beer Street.")

ADDITIONAL INFORMATION

The prints were part of a successful movement to pass legislation governing the sale of liquor. In 1751 the Gin Act was passed. Hogarth was commenting, of course, on social conditions in his day. He was convinced that gin was the curse of the working class, as his own statements show:

> When these two prints were designed and engraved, the dreadful consequences of gin-drinking appeared in every street. In Gin Lane, every circumstance of its horrid effects is brought to view in terrorem. Idleness, poverty, misery, and distress, which drive even to madness and death, are the only objects that are to be seen; and not a house in tolerable condition but the pawnbroker's and Gin-shop.
> Beer Street, its companion, was given as a contrast, where that invigorating liquor is recommended, in order to drive the other out of vogue. Here all is joyous and thriving. Industry and jollity go hand in hand. In this happy place, the pawnbroker's is the only house going to ruin; and even the small quantity of porter that he can procure is taken in at the wicket, for fear of further distress.

After your students have completed their papers they may enjoy comparing their comments with Hogarth's. You will not, of course, expect the students to say approximately what Hogarth said.

Hogarth's paragraphs are quoted in Anecdotes of William Hogarth, facsimile reprint; John Bowyer Nichols, comp. (London: Cornmarket Press, 1970). The following books also give detailed and interesting information about the prints:

> Ronald Paulson, Hogarth: His Life, Art and Times, vol. 2 (New Haven and London: Yale University Press, 1971)

> John Ireland and John Nichols, Hogarth's Works: With Life and Anecdotal Descriptions of His Pictures (London: Chatto & Windus, Publishers, n.d.)

> Engravings by Hogarth: 101 Prints, ed. Sean Shesgreen (New York: Dover Publications, Inc., 1973)

These three books were helpful with several of the less obvious characteristics named in the observations on pages 21-22 above. You may want to refer to them if you decide to spend considerable time on the Hogarth prints.

Hogarth printed at the bottom of each picture a verse appropriate to it. These have been omitted from the text, lest they take

24   Teaching with a Purpose

most of the challenge out of the exercise. You may want to read them to your students after they have finished their work--or during the prewriting if you think they need this sort of help.

For "Gin Lane":

> Gin cursed Fiend, with Fury fraught,
> Makes human Race a Prey;
> It enters by a deadly Draught,
> And steals our Life away.
>
> Virtue and Truth, driv'n to Despair,
> It's Rage compells to fly,
> But cherishes, with hellish Care,
> Theft, Murder, Perjury.
>
> Damn'd Cup! that on the Vitals preys,
> That liquid Fire contains
> Which Madness to the Heart conveys,
> And rolls it thro' the Veins.

For "Beer Street":

> Beer, happy Produce of our Isle
> Can sinewy Strength impart,
> And wearied with Fatigue and Toil
> Can cheer each manly Heart.
>
> Labour and Art upheld by Thee
> Successfully advance,
> We quaff Thy balmy Juice with Glee
> And Water leave to France.
>
> Genius of Health, thy grateful Taste
> Rivals the Cup of Jove,
> And warms each English generous Breast
> With Liberty and Love.

CHAPTER 3   STATING AND OUTLINING A THESIS

Chapter 3 grows naturally out of Chapters 1 and 2. Once students have determined their real subject and purpose and have decided how to get and use material that will enable them to carry out that purpose, they are ready to state a thesis and outline the material that will develop the thesis.

In Chapter 1 your students learned that a real subject is one that has been restricted and that indicates the focus of the paper. The thesis, which McCrimmon defines as "an introductory statement which summarizes the content of an essay by stating the conclusion or main idea to be developed," is a way of stating the real subject. It is not equivalent to a statement of purpose, since purpose includes both the _what_ and the _how_ of an essay, and a thesis states only the _what_, or content, of an essay.

You may need to explain that there is no contradiction between McCrimmon's insistence (1) that a thesis should be arrived at late in the prewriting stage and (2) that it is an introductory statement, to be presented early in the paper. Since the writing stage follows the prewriting stage, it is reasonable that what one has discovered at the end of the prewriting should serve as a beginning for the writing. Furthermore, the thesis almost demands to be near the beginning of the paper; for, as McCrimmon explains, the thesis "notifies the reader what the paper is going to be about, and it reminds the writer what he or she is committed to do."

Beginning teachers of composition will want to give close attention to McCrimmon's explanation that not every paper must have a thesis. At the end of an instructional unit in description, one young instructor made an assignment that required, in addition to vivid description, a thesis. One student wrote about the joy with which a young woman who was unaccustomed to Florida citrus ate an orange that she believed was grown in that state. The paper was marked with an F, with a notation that it contained no thesis. Later that paper, along with others, was used in a study of teachers' grading practices. The grades that most of the eighty-four teachers participating in the study assigned to the paper were A and B. These teachers had not been told that the assignment required a thesis. In one sense, the beginning teacher was right: the paper had no thesis. But it didn't need one, and the request for a thesis should never have been made.

Exercise (page 47)

Snoopy does not yet have any need for an editor, for there is nothing to edit. He has an idea that he wants to develop, but he probably does not have a sufficiently clear notion of what he will emphasize for us to believe he has a real subject. And certainly his purpose is not yet formed: even if he knows what he wants to do, he hasn't decided how he will do it. Snoopy needs to do some thinking before he begins to write.

DERIVING A THESIS FROM YOUR MATERIAL

This section reinforces the point made in Chapter 2 about the importance of arriving at the thesis on the basis of the observations that have been made. In this chapter McCrimmon uses the material about freshman ratings of objectives to emphasize the same method of interpretation that he taught with the Hogarth prints in Chapter 2. The problem he works out here is more complicated than the Hogarth problem; you will need to teach this section very carefully.

One characteristic of the study about the rating of objectives that should be stressed is the reexamination of two theses that seemed to be satisfactory but were actually too simplistic because they ignored important implications suggested by the data. The student who is assumed to be making this study is determined to arrive at a conclusion that accounts for all of the data. When he does eventually arrive at such a conclusion, he realizes that there are two ways of stating the thesis; each way takes into account all of the data. Which of the final two statements he decides to use will depend on what part of his findings he thinks should be emphasized. Most of your students are not accustomed to such a critical examination of conclusions. Here is your chance to make the point that the careful thinker and writer is not satisfied until he or she is convinced that the conclusion to be developed in the paper represents the closest approach to accuracy that he or she can achieve.

Conclusions about "Edith, Christmas A.M." (pages 51-52)

Your students made their observations about Edith, Christmas A.M. when they studied the exercise on pages 31, 32. Now you are asking them to use those observations, or some made from their own perspectives, to determine what theses about the picture are supportable. Remind the students that, though the theses resulting from each observer's thinking about the scene will be influenced by that person's own Christmas morning experiences, all theses should be capable of being supported by evidence in the picture.

Following are some theses that could reasonably emerge from a study of the picture. If you present these to the class, you probably should not do so until the students are well on the way to developing their own theses.

Stating and Outlining a Thesis   27

What took so long to prepare is over so quickly.

I'm glad that next Christmas is a whole year away.

The old room will survive: it has witnessed many such mornings.

Two observers of the same details will often see two remarkably different scenes.

The room in which Christmas morning is celebrated has something in common with a table on which a feast is served: the before-and-after scenes are striking for their contrast.

The Christmas morning festivities are a poor symbol for the birth of the Christ Child.

Discussion Problem (page 52)

The source for this material is presented on page 111, along with a thesis and outline. You may want to refer students to that page <u>after</u> they have completed this exercise.

Physical characteristics

1. Girls and boys are about three inches taller and ten pounds heavier than were youngsters of the same ages in 1920.

3. Because of progress in medicine, childhood diseases that stunt and maim have been largely prevented.

6. Improvements in nutrition and medicine have caused adolescents to mature physiologically much earlier than in the past.

8. In the United States the average age for the onset of puberty has dropped for girls from 14 in 1920 to 12.4 today; for boys it has dropped from 15 to 13.5.

Educational characteristics

2. Investigators have noted that the average American sixteen-year-old has had five years more schooling than his or her counterpart in 1920.

4. The average student today scores approximately one standard deviation above the score of an average student of a generation ago.

5. A level of performance that places a student in the middle of a graduating class today would probably have placed that student in the top 15 percent thirty years ago.

7. A recent U.S. Census Bureau study reveals that the number of young adults with high school diplomas has doubled since 1940.

9. In scholastic achievement teen-agers today are approximately one grade ahead of where their parents were at the same age.

Summarizing statements:

Girls and boys today grow to be larger and experience physical maturation earlier than did young people two generations ago.

The educational achievement of teen-agers exceeds that of teen-agers in their parents' and grandparents' generations.

Possible thesis for a two-paragraph paper

Young people today are more advanced physically and educationally than were their forebears.

GOOD AND BAD THESES

Now that the students have considered how to discover a thesis, this section explains how to state it so that it is restricted, unified, and precise.

Your students may have some difficulty seeing the difference between restriction and unity in a thesis. The two concepts are related, of course. You can help the students distinguish between them by emphasizing that restriction is concerned primarily with scope and size and that unity is concerned primarily with oneness.

Students may erroneously see restricting and unifying a thesis as a new stage in their writing process. Assure them that, instead, it is a continuation of what they began when they settled on a real instead of a general subject. When they check to make certain that a thesis is restricted, they are testing once again, before they begin to write, decisions that they made earlier.

Two kinds of deficiencies in stating theses are common enough to warrant speaking about them. First, students often begin with such expressions as "It will be the purpose of this paper to show that . . ." and "I believe that . . . ." Tell them to omit such expressions and simply to state the basic point that the paper will make. Second, students often write a wordy and grammatically complicated sentence, or even two or more sentences, as a thesis. It is true that professional writers will sometimes state a thesis in more than one sentence, but for beginning writers it is desirable to limit the thesis to a single sentence. That sentence should be as concise and straightforward as possible without sacrificing clarity.

Stating and Outlining a Thesis   29

Discussion Problem (page 55)

Writing a satisfactory thesis requires a degree of intellectual discipline that many students have difficulty practicing. But unless they learn to write good theses, they will be severely handicapped in their composition work. This discussion problem, then, deserves the class's close attention.

One problem that may develop is students' insistence on judging a thesis according to whether they agree with what it says. A student who believes that a thesis is so wrong that no reasonable paper can be developed from it should of course not be discouraged from saying so. But most of the discussion should center on the criteria presented in the text: Is the thesis restricted, unified, and precise? This is a question students are not accustomed to speaking to, and so they may need guidance lest they use valuable class time doing what they feel comfortable doing--talking about what they approve and disapprove of.

A good way to handle this exercise is to begin by simply calling for a vote, without discussion, on which theses are generally acceptable and which are not, and recording the vote on the board. Then, ignoring for the present those theses accepted by majority vote, take up the unacceptable theses one by one and ask for the reasons for rejecting them. Do not comment on these reasons, except to request clarification when necessary and to prevent the discussion from moving to irrelevant matters: let the class agree or disagree with a given reason. If a particular problem causes difficulty, you can ask two or three students to write revised versions of the thesis on the board for discussion. Then repeat the procedure by asking those who voted against the "acceptable" theses to explain why they rejected them.

If you refrain from participating in the discussion, except to moderate, it is probable that the class will reach a consensus on which are the best and worst theses, approving of the appropriate criticism and rejecting the obviously bad criticism and that which is excessive. But even if there is no consensus, they will be involved in a more searching exploration of the theses than will be provided by a "right" or "wrong" fiat by you. When the discussion has run its course, you may want to present your own preferences.

You can compare your judgments about the thesis statements with the evaluations that follow.

Acceptable: 1, 3, 4, 6

Unacceptable for the reasons stated:

2. Interesting is so imprecise that no clear idea emerges. The statement allows the writer to do anything he or she considers "interesting." It neither commits the writer nor informs the reader about what the essay will do. Revision: "During my senior year in high school I enjoyed several trips that

increased my insight into the history and literature our class had been studying."

5. The two sentences and the two main clauses of the second sentence could lead to a lack of unity. Revision: "It is difficult to find housing in desirable locations at reasonable prices."

7. The metaphor is imprecise. Presumably it is intended to mean that we should not assume the success of the conference before we see the results it produces. That meaning can be stated more clearly without the metaphor.

8. The major problem is that <u>should be considered</u> is so imprecise that it conveys no clear meaning to a reader, and perhaps none to the writer. What action does the thesis propose concerning the alleged "evils," and who is to take that action? Revision: "The governing board of the NCAA must make certain that college athletes are amateurs, not well-disguised professionals."

9. This thesis could be developed in two separate parts: the weaknesses of the UN and its inability to prevent a war between major powers. This possible lack of unity could be removed by rewriting the thesis to read "The major weakness of the UN is its inability to prevent a war between major powers" or by restricting it to "The UN cannot prevent a war between major powers."

10. This thesis needs restriction. It proposes to deal with two large topics within a single paper. The simplest way to restrict it is to limit it either to television or to leniency of the courts as a major cause of violence.

OUTLINING A THESIS

When your students are to outline their papers, you will have to decide whether to require topic or sentence outlines. McCrimmon explains that the nature of the paper should determine the kind of outline.

Consider the topic outline on page 56. Suppose it were set up as a sentence outline:

Thesis: I had four reasons for coming to college.

I. I wanted to improve my economic status.
II. I wanted to develop social poise.
III. I wanted to make myself a cultured person.
IV. I wanted to enjoy college activities.

The thesis does not make a statement that must be supported; it merely announces the kind of enumeration that is to follow. (Since the title of the paper will be something similar to "My Reasons for Coming to College," the thesis is almost superfluous.) When the enumeration appears in sentence form, the sentences are conspicuously repetitious. No great harm is done--they are simply not needed.

But using a topic outline when a sentence outline is needed can do damage to the paper. Suppose that the sentence outline on page 56 were written in topic outline form:

>Thesis: The financial benefits of a college education are not so convincing as they used to be.
>
>   I. Employment
>   II. Wages
> III. Costs

This thesis is one that must be supported ("proved," your students may say). If the outline units are stated in sentence form, both writer and reader can tell whether the writer has planned to speak directly to the issue announced by the thesis. If the outline units are written in the form presented above, they give no such guidance. The paper may or may not develop the thesis. (We could write phrases for a topic outline that would be long enough and complex enough to assure us that the outline units would speak to the thesis. But these phrases would be more trouble to write than sentences, and they probably would give less guidance.)

CONSTRUCTING AN OUTLINE

Several problems in outlining are so common that experienced teachers of composition know students must be cautioned against them. Beginning teachers may profit from being alerted to these problems.

>Mixing sentences and nonsentences: remind students that a topic outline should contain no sentences except the thesis and that a sentence outline should not contain any nonsentences.
>
>Listing too many main units or too many subunits under a main unit: the student may be outlining in too much detail, or failure to see that some of the items should be subordinated to others may be the problem.
>
>Overextending the number of subunits, like this:
>
>   I. _____
>   A. _____
>   1. _____
>   a. _____
>   (etc.)

Many freshman papers do not need to be outlined beyond the subunit of the first degree (capital letter). Few need to be outlined beyond the subunit of the second degree (Arabic numeral). Notice that McCrimmon makes this point on pages 57-58 when, for other reasons, he presents an outline that shows more detailed information than is necessary.

Writing outline sentences identical with those in the paper: normally outline sentences should be more concise than most sentences in the paper. If most of the outline sentences are very similar to or identical with those in the paper, and if the paper is outlined in detail, the outline can seem to be an alternate draft of the paper, with numbers and letters added. Such an outline may very well have been written after the paper was finished.

Some students think that the following arrangement is satisfactory as a topic outline.

Thesis: _____.
   I. Introduction
  II. Body
     A. _____
     B. _____
     C. _____
 III. Conclusion

Two criticisms need to be made of this arrangement. First, the main units of the paper should be labeled with Roman numerals, but here the main units (we assume) are listed under <u>Body</u> as subunits. <u>Body</u> should not have a place in the outline. Second, a purely introductory section and a purely concluding section do not need to be outlined. Certainly such sections are not needed in the outline for stating the basic point of the paper: the thesis does that. The introduction-body-conclusion outline may be justifiable in high school writing when a student is receiving his first introduction to outlining, but it is generally unhelpful in college writing.

TESTING AN OUTLINE

Teachers of composition know, of course, that a large percentage of outlines are written after the paper has been written. This practice would not be so harmful as it is if students had the time and inclination to write the paper, construct the outline, discover the faults in the content and organization of the paper, begin over and do their prewriting carefully, write another outline, and then rewrite the paper. But that does not happen often: faults that a student discovers while outlining an already written paper usually remain in the paper.

Even your students who do write outlines before they write their papers are not likely to test the outlines methodically

Stating and Outlining a Thesis 33

unless you make certain that they know how to do that and unless you persuade them that testing outlines will save time and help them write better papers. The discussion problem that concludes this chapter will give you a chance to make the attempt. Your students will subject an outline to McCrimmon's four tests for an outline:

1. Is the thesis satisfactory?

2. Is the relation among the parts clear and consistent?

3. Does the order of the parts provide a logical progression?

4. Is the outline complete?

Discussion Problem (pages 60-61)

1. The use of the word *important* in the thesis is not necessarily objectionable. The problem is that the thesis does not focus on any reason or reasons that college sports are important to the university. The only reason given in the outline is in this sentence: "College sports are great money raisers." A revision of that sentence (to edit out *great*) could be used as a thesis: "College sports raise large amounts of money." So could this one: "College sports are important to the university because they raise large amounts of money." The basic problem concerning the thesis is that it has no opportunity to be satisfactory, since the paper does not focus on any single subject.

2. Only the second main statement and the second half of the fourth main statement speak to the thesis statement.

3. Under I: A is not relevant to I; B is.
   Under II: A is relevant to II; B is not.
   Under III: The relevance of A to III is questionable.
   Under IV: The relevance of A and B to IV is questionable. C is relevant to the second of the two points expressed in IV, "sports improve everyone's social life."

4. A does not develop III adequately. Here are some other possible subtopics:

   --They believe that top administrators give more attention to the quality of the athletic program than to the quality of the academic program.

   --They believe that the emphasis on sports creates an erroneous public opinion of what a university should be.

   --They believe that the emphasis on sports deprives athletes of a college education.

   --They believe that the emphasis on sports leads to dishonest payment of athletes.

But notice that none of these statements can support the thesis, for III does not support it.

5. One cannot determine the real subject, since both restriction and focus are lacking. The fault is the writer's.

6. The outline is unsatisfactory as a plan on which to base a paper. It fails to satisfy any of the four criteria given for testing an outline.

7. The instructor's outline shows very clearly that the organization of the paper is not satisfactory.

8. and 9. Ideally, of course, the student should have developed a thesis and outline in his prewriting. (One suspects that he did little prewriting but did his preliminary thinking as he wrote.) The next best plan would have been for him to outline his rough draft. That outline would have revealed his problems in organization. (His rough draft was probably quite similar to his "finished" draft.)

10. As your students respond to this question, you will probably be able to discover whether some of them have been convinced of the advantage of doing their prewriting carefully, including writing and testing a thesis and an outline.

CHAPTER 4   COMMON PATTERNS OF DEVELOPMENT

The first three chapters deal with fundamental prewriting problems: determining purpose, finding a real subject, deciding what to say about a subject, discovering and stating a thesis, and organizing an outline that will develop a thesis. Chapter 4 is an extension of the outlining section of Chapter 3: it teaches some basic patterns of developing ideas. This chapter completes the prewriting section of the text.

Though you may ask students to develop whole papers using one controlling pattern of development, you should make sure they understand that a writer may use more than one pattern in an essay, that a section of a paper may be developed by whatever pattern is needed at a particular place. Essays in the "Common Patterns of Development" chapter will make this point. First, the paper that contrasts different concepts of time in American and non-Western societies (page 67) relies heavily on illustration. Second, though the paragraph about computers and the human brain (page 69) progresses by the A/B pattern of comparison and contrast, within the paragraph is this example of the "how-it-works" process:

> . . . the machine operates linearly, that is, it sends an impulse of "thought" along one path, so that if that path proves to be a dead end the "thought" must back up to the last fork in the road and try again, and if the "thought" is derailed the whole process must be begun again; the brain operates in some mysterious multipath fashion whereby a thought apparently splits and moves along several different paths simultaneously so that no matter what happens to any one of its branches there are others groping along.

Finally, the causal process paper about the decay of the cities (pages 82-83) closes with a quotation that illustrates what mayors were thinking about the plight of the large city. You want your students to master each pattern of development, of course; but be sure they understand that each does not have to stand alone--that patterns can work side by side, or even one within another.

ILLUSTRATION

To emphasize to your students the usefulness of illustration, you can explain that it occurs naturally in our speech. Time after time when we fear that we are being unclear we say, "For example, ..." We also use illustration when we sense that we are speaking well and want to make a point especially clear by supporting it with a good story. In fact, we may take such pleasure in narrating the illustration that we look for a chance to make the point just so we can tell the story. It is ironic, then, that illustration, the very device that we use so spontaneously and pleasurably in speech, is so often missing in writing. Remind your students that illustration is a method of development that can serve them as well in their writing as in their speech.

One common problem in the use of illustration occurs when the example is not quite applicable to the point being made. You may find the following paragraph useful as you talk to your students about this problem.

> Sometimes children's fear of being rejected prevents them from telling their friends of their affection. This fear is especially strong in little boys experiencing early "puppy" love. I still remember how trembly I felt when Jeannie smiled at me during our second-grade music lesson. At recess that day I gave her three sweaty M&M's and told her that she was my sweetheart. She ate the candy quickly.

The topic sentence of the paragraph speaks of situations in which children do not tell other children of their affection, but in the example the child does profess his. The topic sentence speaks of the fear of being rejected, but in the example Jeannie has smiled at the little boy. Perhaps the boy almost did not tell Jeannie that she was his sweetheart, and perhaps he did feel that she might reject him (he was "trembly"); but these feelings are not part of the illustration.

Another matter that will require your attention is the TRI system of analysis, which McCrimmon emphasizes in this edition. Although a TRI analysis is a simple method of showing the structure of some paragraphs, it does sometimes present problems that need discussion. For example, in the paragraph on pages 65-66, some students may have two difficulties. First, they may not recognize that sentence 3 is not a specific example of the topic sentence but a clarifying statement that makes the meaning of the topic sentence clearer and so should be marked R. Second, they may wonder whether the shark and lizard examples should be marked as one illustration or two--that is, as I or as I_1 and I_2.

In dealing with such problems, the main point to emphasize is that the TRI method is designed to show the general structure of the paragraph as a whole and is not intended to emphasize the function of each sentence in the paragraph. The simplest analysis merely identifies the three parts. In this particular paragraph sentences 4 and 5 both belong in the part marked I. There is no objection to marking sentence 4 as I_1 and sentence 5 as I_2. But if a paragraph has a long series of examples, each of which is presented in a single sentence, labeling every example with a different subscript makes the analysis more precise than it needs to be and encourages students to look at individual sentences rather than at the basic TRI pattern. The simplest analysis of the paragraph developing the claim that "the biologically good die young" is TRIT.

Some students may object that sentence 3 is also an illustration and therefore should be marked I, not R. This is a sensible objection and should not be hastily dismissed. The best way to handle it is to ask the class whether this is a specific illustration, like those of the sharks and lizards, or a general statement about many animals and thus a clarification of the topic sentence rather than a specific example. The class consensus is likely to be that sentence 3 should be marked R rather than I; but dissenters are entitled to their opinions, and their dissent will force the whole class to look more carefully at the problem.

Discussion Problem (page 66)

The simplest analysis of the paragraph about young Arthur is 1----T, 2----R, 3-8----I, 9----T. But since this is a two-part contrast of the A+B pattern described on pages 67-68, it would be useful to point up the structure of the contrast by making the ants and the geese separate, contrasting illustrations. If this is done, the following pattern will describe the structure:

1----T
2----R
3-5----I_1
6-8----I_2
9----T

COMPARISON

Students sometimes have difficulty at first seeing the distinction between the divided pattern and the alternating pattern of comparison and contrast. You can help them distinguish between the patterns by asking them to think of one major part of the subject matter as item A and the other major part as item B. The divided pattern proceeds item by item--that is, all of item A and then all of item B (A+B). In the alternating pattern the points to be made about the two items are taken up point by point. The two items are usually discussed in adjacent sentences or within the same sentence. As each point is being explained, item A and item B are both discussed; and so in the point-by-point explanation the discussion continually alternates between A and B (A/B, A/B, A/B). If you will explain carefully how you are using the symbols A+B and A/B, you can spare your students a good deal of unnecessary confusion.

The outlines on page 70 should be helpful as you make your explanation.

To make sure your students understand the two patterns before they begin to write papers using comparison and contrast, you could have them make outlines based on the first two paragraphs about one's body and a car (page 68) that are similar to the outlines of the discussion of a computer and the brain (pages 69-70). Your students' outlines will look like this:

<u>Alternating Pattern</u>

A/B 1 Consuming fuel
       Body (food)
       Car (gasoline)

A/B 2 Converting fuel
       to energy
       Body
       Car

A/B 3 Using energy and
       emitting waste
       Body
       Car

A/B 4 Storing energy
       Body (yes)
       Car (no)

<u>Divided Pattern</u>

A. Body
1. Consuming fuel (food)
2. Converting fuel to energy
3. Using energy and emitting waste
4. Storing energy (yes)

B. Car
1. Consuming fuel (gasoline)
2. Converting fuel to energy
3. Using energy and emitting waste
4. Storing energy (no)

The text points out that neither of the patterns is better than the other for all purposes. There are some precautions that a writer should be aware of when choosing which method to use. Sometimes a student who intends to use the divided pattern will write two separate discussions without making the comparison clear to the reader, even though it exists in the writer's mind. If the subject matter permits, this effect can be avoided by giving care to the arrangement of the parts of A and B. Notice that in the A+B outline (page 70) of the computer and brain paragraph the discussion of speed appears first in both A and B, the discussion of path of thought appears second in both A and B, and so on. The structure, then, helps to hold the two basic parts of the discussion together. The same kind of observation can be made by studying the divided-pattern outline presented just above for the comparison of the human body and a car. Another problem with the divided pattern is the writer's tendency to repeat much of the information about A when comparing B with A. The divided pattern is likely to work most satisfactorily in a short discussion and with a subject where the comparison can be implied.

Most comparative papers that college students write are sufficiently long and complex to warrant the use of the alternating, or point-by-point, pattern. The problem to avoid in using this pattern is jumping back and forth from A to B so quickly and so often that the reader has the sensation of watching a Ping-Pong game. If the writer does not see a way to avoid this problem, the divided pattern may be preferable.

A question that should arise in your prewriting instruction for comparison and contrast is whether a paper can be all comparison or all contrast. The answer, of course, is yes. But a paper that only contrasts is likely to be most justifiable and interesting if it deals with two items that seem to be almost identical; a paper that merely compares could well be about two items that seem to be very different. If one can show how a liberal arts program differs from a general education program, the contrast will add to the reader's knowledge on a significant subject. If a writer can show that a car and a human body have a great deal in common (pages 68-69), that discussion will deserve and probably get the reader's attention.

Still another question may arise. Aren't comparison and contrast on the one hand and classification on the other just about the same? No--though certainly there are similarities. The writer who would compare and contrast has to be aware of the class or classes to which the items belong. And the writer who classifies must know that the items being classified have similarities and differences. It is a matter of focus and purpose, then. A writer whose purpose requires the use of classification will focus on grouping items into classes and subclasses according to their similar traits; one whose purpose requires comparison and contrast will concentrate on showing similarities and differences between the items. The writer should be aware that the two patterns of organization are related, but each has its own forms and uses.

Exercise A (page 70)

Though the A+B pattern does not demand that the details of item B be discussed in the same order as the details of item A, the cartoon material does lend itself to that arrangement. Such an arrangement can contribute to (but will not automatically create) the effect of a unified comparison rather than that of two separate discussions.

Most of the following details will probably be cited in your students' papers.

Part A:

1. Hair--Both people wear long hair. Hers is very straight.

2. Glasses--His glasses are styled after old-fashioned spectacles, with oval shape and wire frames. Hers are large, round spectacles. The styles were popular with young women in the early 1970s.

3. Clothes--He wears a T-shirt under a military-type field jacket that has an insignia on the right shoulder. She wears a shirt

(with the shirt tail outside her trousers) over a T-shirt (printed with school letters?). She appears to be braless. Both wear bell-bottom trousers, and both wear sandals, without socks.

4. Method of carrying items--His large field jacket pockets and her large shoulder bag (with fringes) have room enough for them to carry just about whatever they want to. The pockets and the bag seem to be full.

5. Body position and movement--He embraces her with his left arm. His right hand seems to be reaching out for something. She has her hands behind her (probably clasped). Both are walking with long, carefree strides, probably rapidly.

6. Facial expressions--Both are smiling broadly. She seems to be attentive to what he is saying.

7. What is said--They are pleased with today and are anticipating tomorrow with pleasure.

Part B:

1. Hair--Both wear short hair. His is combed neatly, and hers is waved stylishly.

2. Glasses--The frames of his glasses are dark and moderately thick. Her frames have a pointed, stylish shape.

3. Clothes--He wears a dress shirt, a tie, and a conservative business suit. His black leather shoes are shined. (A pipe complements his conservative dress.) She wears a scarf tie under the jacket of her neatly tailored woman's suit.

4. Method of carrying items--There is no room in their pockets or in her conservative purse for bulky items. The couple has a baby stroller designed to carry their twins.

5. Body position and movement--He embraces her with his left arm. His right arm reaches out to the baby stroller and the twins. She has one hand in her jacket pocket and holds her purse with one hand. They seem to be walking slowly.

6. Facial expressions--Both have worried expressions. She seems to be attentive to what he is saying.

7. What is said--They seem to dread the arrival of tomorrow.

CLASSIFICATION

Many students never understand classification. If they are required to write papers in which they must use this pattern of organization, they often break the subject into selected parts that interest them and discuss each part, or they may simply make a list of related items and discuss each item on the list. Instructors, frustrated over what they can say that will enable students to understand this pattern that seems so simple, are sometimes tempted to mark the papers for spelling, punctuation, and other routine matters and move on to the next unit. Because McCrimmon is aware of the difficulty teachers have in teaching this pattern of organization, he explains classification very carefully.

Early in the explanation McCrimmon begins a demonstration by classifying words according to how their meanings have changed. When your students have discussed all the words and have completed the classifying, they will have set up these groups:

Toward broader meaning	Toward narrower meaning
arrive	eaves
butcher	hound
cupboard	liquor
dismantle	rose
frock	starve
target	voyage

Toward less favorable meaning	Toward more favorable meaning
boor	count
cad	marshal
crafty	nice
prude	shrewd
silly	steward
villain	
wench	

You have observed that the text advocates the inductive approach to classification. But you should not assume that the students will make the same observation, for most of them will be considering the subject for the first time. As you summarize their work with the twenty-four words, emphasize that they approached a body of unorganized material, analyzed it, and then grouped the data into classes. Once the students understand this disciplined concept of classification, they should begin to see how this pattern of organization can serve them as writers who know what they want to do and how they want to do it.

On "The Four Faces of New York"

Obviously the paragraphs about the faces of New York (pages 76-78) did not develop in exactly the same way as would a paragraph about the kinds of word change demonstrated by the twenty-four examples. The individual items from which the classes are developed in the article about New York do not exist in simple, clear-cut entities. But the basic principle is the same: as McCrimmon points out, the writer knew details about New York's history that allowed him to arrange these details into classes that he chose to call faces. The following material is an abbreviated account of the information from which he formed the classes.

First face--port city (dating from nineteenth century)

Caused by:
- ideal harbor
- commerce between (1) American West and (2) American East and Europe
- railroads and canals connecting New York with West
- concentration of business establishments necessary for trade

Influence of port on nature of city:
- concentration of port-associated businesses in downtown New York
- disreputable sections near port
- large number of immigrants

Second face--manufacturing city (dating from beginning of twentieth century)

Extent of manufacturing:
- "40,000 manufacturing establishments"
- almost 1,000,000 industrial workers
- "largest manufacturing payroll . . . of any American city"

Nature of manufacturing:
- garment
- printing and publishing
- specialized small firms that provide items needed by manufacturers

Third face--corporate headquarters city (dating from early 1950s)

Reversal of trend for corporations to leave New York
Large number of new office buildings
Headquarters for many large industrial corporations
Service firms for corporations

Fourth face--cultural city (dating from mid-1960s)

Long-time cultural institutions (background for new emphasis):
- publishing firms
- universities
- museums (including art collections)
- art galleries
- dramatic theaters
- music and dance productions

Reasons for new emphasis on culture:
- establishment of United Nations in New York
- desire of young businessmen and executives for cultural attractions
- desire of middle-class descendants of immigrants (particularly Jews) for cultural attractions
- creation of Lincoln Square (for performing arts)
- expansion of undergraduate and graduate education (growth of Columbia University and New York University)

Common Patterns of Development   43

Exercise A (page 78)

Here are three ways in which the sports can be classified. Your students will probably think of others.

According to degree of physical contact

Heavy	Some	None
boxing	baseball	golf
football	basketball	gymnastics
hockey		swimming
soccer		tennis
wrestling		track

According to whether a ball or similar object is used

Yes	No
baseball	boxing
basketball	gymnastics
football	swimming
golf	track
hockey	wrestling
soccer	
tennis	

According to whether a batlike instrument is used

Yes	No
baseball	basketball
golf	boxing
hockey	football
tennis	gymnastics
	soccer
	swimming
	track
	wrestling

Exercise B (page 78)

When you make the assignment called for by this exercise, you will need to stress that the details from which the classes are formed should appear in the paragraphs, as they do in "The Four Faces of New York." A narrative that tells about the student's riding down the main street on a parade float in one paragraph and explains in another paragraph that the block where her dentist's office was located was a fearful section of town for her will not fulfill the assignment—unless she has set out to classify sections of her town according to the impressions that her experiences in the sections made on her. Nor will the assignment about teaching procedures be satisfied by personality profiles of the teacher whom the student liked most and the one she disliked most. Ask your students to make sure they know what the assignment calls for, then to list as many details as they can that are relevant to the topic, and then to ask into what classes the details will allow themselves to be grouped. This procedure need not rule out the addition of details that come to mind after the classes have begun to form. The procedure should enable students to write classification papers, not papers that merely narrate or describe or compare.

PROCESS

Exercise (page 83)

One reason for having your students write a process essay is that this kind of assignment lends itself to emphasizing clarity. If a paper that is supposed to tell how to do something or how something works or how a cause produces an effect is not clear, its flaw is immediately apparent to the reader. If the reader doesn't understand, the writer can definitely determine what to do to be clear. For these reasons, having students read each other's drafts before the finished copies come to you can be particularly helpful.

Another advantage of this assignment is that you can easily show that the audience is a strong determiner of what needs to be said. The instructions stipulate that the reader is not familiar with the subject matter. The writer has to consider carefully what will be clear: "Can I use the term cross-court volley in explaining how a tennis player takes advantage of having rushed to the net?" "Can I say north-northeast in giving directions?" "Can I assume that my reader will understand elementary terminology from chemistry as I explain how gasoline burns in an engine and produces energy?"

You should emphasize that a process paper requires that the writer give particular attention to order. The outlines of the essays about map reading (pages 79-81) and of the causes for the dying of cities (pages 82-83) show how clearly an outline can point up the stages in a process. Call these outlines to the attention of your students if you want to recommend that they use a simple outline to make sure that the sequence of events is clear and logical.

A student who writes a causal-process paper will have to do more than just make sure that the sequence of events is correct. He will have to ask whether an event that preceded another caused the second. Chanticleer was mistaken when he concluded that his crowing caused the sun to rise. What the coach told the quarterback during a time-out period may have caused the touchdown play: perhaps he had spotted a weakness in the opponent's defense and told the quarterback how to take advantage of it. But his instructions may not have caused the touchdown: perhaps the quarterback changed the play by an audible signal when he saw the defensive alignment, or perhaps the running back ran the wrong pattern and scored in spite of his mistake. If a writer is to explain a causal process, it is not enough simply to establish a sequence of events, to show that the coach talked to the quarterback and then the team scored.

DEFINITION

Early in his discussion of definition McCrimmon explains and gives examples of two kinds of definition: short and stipulative. Students may need some help from you with the second. Though they may not be familiar with the adjective <u>stipulative</u>, most do know the verb <u>stipulate</u>. You can explain, then, that a stipulative definition stipulates what a term means in a particular situation. Be sure to stress the stipulative definition that is basic in the text, that in our study <u>purpose</u> means "the basic commitments writers make when determining (1) what they want to do, and (2) how they want to do it." Obviously this definition is quite different from a short definition of <u>purpose</u>, which might be "aim" or "intention."

Because the kind of definition that receives most attention in composition courses is extended definition, this is the kind the text emphasizes. Two examples of extended definition and brief analyses of them are followed by practical advice about writing such a paper.

McCrimmon emphasizes that there is no particular pattern to which an extended definition must conform, that the writer may use whatever pattern or patterns of development are useful as he or she explains what something means. The definition of a limerick relies heavily on illustration, and the definition of the "Definitions" game is also a process paper. You might remind your students of William Faulkner's explanation that a writer, like a carpenter, uses whatever tool he needs to get a particular part of the job done and that different tools are needed at different times in the job.

<u>Exercises</u> (page 89)

Exercise A can be the basis for a lively class discussion. Students should enjoy presenting, perhaps even developing, definitions of terms about which no dictionary has spoken. There are no "correct" or "incorrect" answers--except, possibly, those that are accepted or rejected by most people who hear the definitions. Give the students rein to explain why they accept or reject particular definitions. Don't rule out stipulative definitions, but when one is presented make sure that the students know what kind of definition they are discussing.

When the students are preparing for Exercise B, encourage them to choose subjects about which they care enough to want to explain them to other people. Definitions that are written for no reason other than fulfilling an assignment can be extremely dull.

McCrimmon encourages students to rely on their own thinking and experience as they define. When they do this, their discussions may occasionally drift into discourse that is questionable as definition. But be gentle with and encouraging to the students as long as they are concentrating on trying to explain the meaning of the subject. Don't set up such rigid requirements and penalties that the students dare not take chances. Those who do take chances and succeed are likely to write the very best papers you receive.

PART 2

WRITING AND REWRITING

CHAPTER 5   PARAGRAPHS: UNITS OF DEVELOPMENT

In the first four chapters McCrimmon is concerned primarily with teaching the process of prewriting an essay and showing how the prewriting affects the writing. The chapter on paragraphs begins the "Writing and Rewriting" section of the text. In this and the following chapters the emphasis is on what happens in the writing process itself: in developing paragraphs, structuring sentences, choosing exactly the right words, and finding an appropriate style.

This section of the text also teaches revision, a kind of writing with which students have had little experience. There is something very final about committing words to paper; few students are eager to revise in any significant way what they have written, nor do they know without instruction how to go about it. You will have to emphasize repeatedly that revising is much more than just correcting errors in spelling, punctuation, grammar, and usage; for many, perhaps most, of your students will consider revision to be merely correction, not a process of criticizing and rewriting a piece.

DEVELOPING TOPICAL PARAGRAPHS

McCrimmon divides paragraphs into two categories: (1) topical--those that develop the ideas the paper presents, and (2) special--those that introduce, provide transition, and conclude. He discusses topical paragraphs by subjecting models to four tests: for unity, completeness, order of movement, and coherence.

UNITY

The material on unity asks the student to consider how unity is maintained in one model paragraph and why it is lacking in two other paragraphs. In the paragraph about the Roman Empire, each sentence has a relationship to the topic sentence. In the paragraph about Pompeii, there is evidence that the writer had not settled on one topic idea before she wrote. And in the paragraph about college writing, we can determine where the writer began to stray from his topic sentence and can observe the result--a contradiction of what he set out to say. When you are discussing the material on unity, concentrate not on the mere presence or absence of unity but on <u>how</u> and <u>why</u> the paragraphs pass or fail the test for unity.

The discussion of unity emphasizes that the writer can bring unity to the paragraph by determining clearly what the topic idea is and then keeping it in mind. Continual reference to the topic idea or topic sentence will serve you well in your instruction, just as does reference to the thesis when you are speaking of the unity of the whole essay. You will want to emphasize the value that the topic sentence has not only as a guide in the writing process, but also as a checking device during revision: McCrimmon advises the student that "if you should drift into inconsistencies, at least you have a standard by which to judge the paragraph during revision" (page 98).

<u>Discussion Problem</u> (page 97)

The first sentence of the paragraph suggests that the focus will be on the itinerant street preacher, and sentences 2 and 3 reinforce this suggestion. The shift in focus begins in sentence 4, when the writer speaks of the locations of the audience. One of these locations, the bank steps, captures the writer's interest, and the rest of the paragraph speaks of the bank steps as a place where people traditionally gathered to talk on Saturday afternoons. The preacher has been edged out of the paragraph.

The two obvious options open to the writer are (1) to keep the focus on the preacher or (2) to write about the significance of the bank steps in the life of the community. If he chooses the first, sentence 4 may still have a place in the paragraph, for it can lead into a section of the paragraph that tells still more about the preacher by showing how he addresses the several parts of the audience. Separate paragraphs focusing on the preacher and the bank steps would be appropriate in a paper that discusses characteristics of "small Southern towns a generation ago."

This discussion problem can help you to show how subtly lack of unity can mar a paragraph. Normally the writer of such a paragraph does not see that there is any break in the train of thought. In the writer's mind each sentence grows, or seems to grow, out of the one preceding it. Your close attention to this discussion problem and to the faulty paragraphs that precede it can help your students become more sensitive to why and how writers sometimes fail to achieve unity in paragraphs.

<u>Completeness</u>

McCrimmon begins his discussion of completeness by explaining that whether a paragraph is complete depends on whether it gives as much information as the reader needs. What is sufficiently complete for a reader who is already knowledgeable about the subject probably will not be complete for one who is reading about the subject for the first time. You may want to ask your students to read again the section in Chapter 1 called "Your View of Your Reader."

Paragraphs: Units of Development   51

Whatever technique you use, stress the influence that the nature of the audience for whom the paper is intended has on the writing.

You may want to show your students the effect of a series of incomplete paragraphs. If each paragraph lacks specifics to support the generalization, the reader is likely to lose confidence in the writer while moving from one unsubstantiated conclusion to another. You can illustrate this problem by asking your students to compare the following version of the discussion of physical and intellectual traits of young people with the more complete version on page 111.

> Disgruntled souls who shake their heads and mutter that young people aren't what they used to be are, as a matter of fact, absolutely correct. Young people have changed appreciably, and not just in the more publicized and superficial ways.
> Physically, young people are larger and healthier than they were fifty years ago. Advances in nutrition and medicine have caused adolescents to mature physiologically much earlier than in the past.
> Today's young people differ intellectually as well as physically. The average student today scores approximately one standard deviation above the student of a generation ago.

Readers will want to know the evidence that suggests the physiological superiority of young people today. Also many readers will need an explanation of the significance of an increase of a standard deviation in test scores on intellectual development. The original paragraphs give the information that will make the discussion complete for the nonspecialist reader for whom it was written.

Exercise (page 100)

The problem here is that the paragraph stops with the expression of the topic idea. The students are asked to develop the idea by presenting a sustained illustration. Here is how one writer developed the topic idea. This paragraph can serve as a model in your prewriting work with the exercise.

> To excel in any skill, talent alone is not enough. Every kind of worthwhile activity has its special technique. I saw this point illustrated when I was playing basketball my last year in high school. My best friend, who was the captain of our team, is favored with quickness of movement and with an ideal build for a guard. In our junior year he relied mostly on his talent and desire, and he had a moderately good season. But a new coach in our senior year saw that the talent was largely going to waste and set up a training program. Hour after hour the coach would have me try to take the ball from my friend as he dribbled it with his right hand,

protecting the ball from me with his body and left
arm just the way the coach showed him. And, with
instruction, my friend so mastered the feint and
change of pace that he could have me moving to his
left when he would suddenly burst straight in for
a lay-up shot. That year he was named Most Valuable
Player in the state semi-finals. I learned from
this experience that one whose aim is to excel at
a skill needs both talent and technical proficiency.

You can develop an interesting follow-up session on this exercise if you will ditto and let the class discuss several of the students' paragraphs that illustrate satisfactory ways of bringing completeness to the paragraph.

ORDER

The material on paragraph order may strike your students as quite simple. It should, for ideally the movement of a paragraph from beginning to end should seem so natural that its order is obviously the organization that is needed.

General to Particular

McCrimmon discusses first the most commonly taught paragraph order, movement from the topic sentence to the details that support it. The model paragraph that he uses gives the student more experience with the TRIT method of organization (introduced in Chapter 4). The sentences can be labeled like this:

Sentence 1----------T
Sentence 2----------R
Sentences 3-12------I
Sentence 13---------T

This would be an opportune time to remind your students of what they learned in Chapter 2 about basing conclusions on observed data. Though the conclusion in a general-to-particular paragraph appears first, it should be decided on only after the data has been examined.

Particular to General

The form of the particular-to-general paragraph illustrates the inductive order of meaning, of course: the conclusion is presented only after consideration of the particulars.

When your students are deciding whether to use this order, they should ask themselves, "Will withholding the conclusion until the end of the paragraph cause my reader to be confused about where the paragraph is going?" If the answer is no, the particular-to-general order can serve the writer well. But remind your students to ask the question. This order should be used deliberately, not by happenstance.

Whole to Parts

You can build a brief writing exercise and a discussion session around the opening sentences for partitive paragraphs given on page 102. The following paragraph, based on one of those sentences, can be helpful in your prewriting work:

> I have two objections to the proposal that Coach Starnes should not be employed for a third year. First, he has experienced his mediocre won-lost record with players most of whom were recruited by his predecessor. We will not see until next season a team made up primarily of players he recruited and coached from the beginning of their college careers. Second, and even more important, to fire a coach whose only major fault has been not winning almost all of his games is to approve the attitude that all that matters in college athletics is winning. If that attitude wins, our college will be the loser.

McCrimmon points out that a partitive paragraph that would not be sufficient for a complete discussion of a topic can serve well as an introduction. The paragraph that he cites about the requirements for good paragraphs is an example. Another illustration of a partitive paragraph used as an introduction is the one about prewriting, writing, and rewriting on page 4 of the text.

Question to Answer, Effect to Cause

The question-to-answer movement is quite elementary: a question is asked, and an answer is given. If a question arises in class about whether a paragraph that moves from question to answer must also demonstrate movement from effect to cause, the answer is no: it may or may not. But the two kinds of movement are sufficiently related to justify discussing them side by side in the text.

As you discuss movement from effect to cause, you can remind the students of their consideration of causal process in Chapter 4 and the short essay that they read there about the decay of the cities. The order of movement is even more conspicuous now that they are seeing it at work within a single paragraph.

This is not the time to go into detail about causal reasoning. You will do that when you work with the argument section of Chapter 9, "Persuasion." The elementary work in cause-and-effect reasoning that you do now should prove helpful when you and your students consider the more complex material later.

Other Orders of Movement

The orders of paragraph movement in the text are basic. You may prefer to mention no others. But if you decide to discuss chronological order, you can cite these examples in the text:

--the directions for getting through town to the writer's home (page 7)

--in "Three Points of View" (pages 20-22), the first two paragraphs

--in "Where Are You?" (pages 79-81), the paragraphs beginning "One way is to spread the map out . . ." and "To find one's place . . . the first thing to do . . ."

--the explanation of how the female mosquito takes in animal blood (pages 81-82)

And you may decide to introduce your class to spatial order, which may move from left to right, from bottom to top, from near to far--or the reverse of these. But spatial order can also locate the narrator in a particular spot as he or she describes the surroundings in an orderly sequence. The following paragraph from a letter written by a person living in Hawaii does this:

> Our house is high on a mountain ridge. Our ears pop going up and again going down. I'm sitting on the deck of the house now. To the right I look <u>down</u> onto Diamond Head. To the left I look <u>down</u> on Koko Head. Straight ahead is a steep green slope down to a valley with two rows of houses along the bottom. The other side of the valley facing me is untouched vegetation. Across that ridge I can see the palm-lined coast, with waves always breaking white on the coral reef off shore. Up here there is always a cool breeze, and on this deck I usually wear a sweater. Farther up this ridge the clouds usually hide the peaks, and often sudden showers appear there though the sun shines here. Every day we see rainbows, usually full arcs with pots of gold at both ends.

Coherence

Many students have a vague notion of what coherence is, but they have little idea of how to achieve it. The section on coherence in this chapter can help you remedy this problem, for it treats in detail various ways of developing coherence within and among paragraphs. After presenting a demonstration of the problem that lack of coherence causes in a paragraph and of ways to solve the problem, McCrimmon treats the following methods of achieving coherence:

1. through pronoun reference

2. through repetitive structure

3. through contrasted elements

4. through transitional markers

5. through connections between paragraphs

The material on Jefferson as a scholar (pages 105-107) may be quite challenging for some of your students, but it can be particularly helpful if you will go over it carefully with the class. Here we are given a paragraph with faulty coherence, a critique of the faults, a revised coherent version of the paragraph, and a summary of the improvements. This material can help you to talk specifically about characteristics that bring coherence to a paragraph. Also, you can bring specificity to your discussion by citing exact places in the revised paragraph that cause the passage to cohere by showing <u>why</u> Jefferson proceeded as he did. For example:

--sentence 2:   <u>To compare the evidence</u> . . . .

--sentence 3:   the entire sentence

--sentence 4:   <u>To ensure that reason rather than the authority of tradition would guide him</u> . . . .

--sentence 5:   <u>Accordingly</u> . . . .

The Jefferson material also gives you a chance to make an important point about one cause of problems in coherence--that they often develop because the connecting ideas in the writer's mind do not appear on the page. For the writer of the faulty version of the paragraph on Jefferson, the material probably held together and made sense. But the reader, who does not already know what connections the writer had in mind, has trouble. Here is another opportunity for you to emphasize audience analysis and the importance of the writer's considering what the reader needs to be told.

<u>Discussion Problem</u> (pages 107-108)

The establishment of coherence through pronoun reference is perfectly obvious in the marked paragraph about kudzu--so obvious that students may wonder whether the principle needs to be taught. But when they see a paragraph that lacks coherence because the principle has been ignored, their question should be answered. This discussion problem presents such a paragraph.

The paragraph in the second column is a revision of the one in the first column. The weakness of the original paragraph is its lack of coherence, caused partly by the shifting focus from sentence to sentence. Notice the variety of grammatical subjects of the main clauses: sentence 1, <u>students</u>; 2, <u>work</u>; 3, <u>failure</u>;

4, <u>students</u>; 5, <u>to begin . . . and to plunge</u>; 6, <u>habit</u>; 7, <u>students</u>; 8, <u>to quote</u>; 9, <u>notes</u>. But in the second paragraph the focus remains on the students. The phrase <u>many students</u> is the subject of the first main clause; in the following sentences the deliberate repetition of <u>they</u> helps to control the focus. Students will see these relationships very clearly if they will draw lines from <u>students</u> to the pronouns for which <u>students</u> is the referent.

Here is further evidence of the superiority of the coherence of the second paragraph. Sentence 4 in the second paragraph expresses clearly and concisely a relationship between sentences 4 and 5 that is not altogether clear in the first paragraph. In the first paragraph sentences 6 and 7 are related, as are sentences 8 and 9, but the reader has to pause momentarily to determine these relationships. In the second paragraph sentence 5 makes these two sets of associations immediately clear and also establishes a relationship among all four sentences by beginning with "They take more notes than necessary because . . ." and then giving in concise form all the information contained in the four sentences of the other paragraph.

<u>Exercise A</u> (page 110)

By combining sentences that depend on each other for their meaning, varying sentence structure to avoid abruptness and monotony, and using particular words to provide transition and show other logical relationships, we can remedy the lack of coherence in the flawed paragraph. Here is one version of a new paragraph. Explanations of the changes follow the paragraph.

> (<u>A</u>) I was accepted and started work. (<u>B</u>) But because my experience had been derived chiefly from books, I was not prepared for the difficult period of adjustment. (<u>C</u>) Soon I became so discouraged with myself and so dissatisfied with my job that I was on the point of quitting. (<u>D</u>) However, after my employer called me into his office and talked to me about the duties of my position and the opportunities for advancement, I realized there was nothing wrong with me or the job. (<u>E</u>) Therefore I decided to stay.

Sentence A: Same as sentence 1.

Sentence B: Combines sentences 2 and 3. <u>Because</u> helps to establish the relationship between 1 and 2, and <u>but</u> provides transition between A and B.

Sentence C: Combines sentences 4, 5, and 6. <u>Soon</u> has been moved to the head of the sentence to provide transition. The two uses of <u>so</u> and the use of <u>that</u> show the relation of sentences 4 and 5 to sentence 6.

Sentence D: Combines sentences 7, 8, 9, and 10. <u>However</u> provides transition from C to D. Sentences 7, 8, and 9 have

Paragraphs: Units of Development   57

been grouped into one subordinate clause; <u>after</u> helps to establish the relationship between that clause and the main clause, formerly sentence 10.

Sentence E: Same as sentence 11, except that <u>therefore</u> provides transition from D to E.

<u>Exercise B</u> (page 110)

Your students will produce various versions of the paragraph, of course. In your follow-up discussion on the exercise you may be able to use the following version and the detailed explanations of how the changes bring coherence to the original paragraph.

(<u>A</u>) Heavy snow is a rarity in exceptionally cold weather. (<u>B</u>) We can understand why by considering the climatic conditions that are necessary for the forming of snow. (<u>C</u>) Snowflakes can form when the temperature falls below 32° Fahrenheit, for under these conditions wet particles mat together. (<u>D</u>) As the temperature falls still lower, the air dries out; therefore, powder-like particles, not flakes, form. (<u>E</u>) At temperatures below zero snow changes to fine, glittering ice-dust. (<u>F</u>) Because the air under such conditions is usually too dry for snowflakes to form, heavy snowfall seldom occurs at very cold temperatures.

Sentence A: Announces the topic. Has been added to the paragraph.

Sentence B: Restricts the scope of the topic sentence by showing that the paragraph will explain why the topic statement is true. Has been added to the paragraph.

Sentence C: Begins the pattern of references to falling temperature. Combines sentences 1 and 3 in the original paragraph by moving from effect to cause. (Though the old sentence 2 is not part of the new sentence, its meaning is expressed implicitly.)

Sentence D: Contributes to the paragraph's coherence by continuing the pattern of references to falling temperature and combining sentences 4 and 5 in the original paragraph through movement from cause to effect. <u>Therefore</u> serves as a transitional word.

Sentence E: Contributes to the paragraph's coherence by continuing, implicitly, the cause-and-effect reasoning utilized in sentences C and D.

Sentence F: Combines sentences 8 and 7 in the original paragraph through cause-to-effect order. Restates the topic idea.

58 Teaching with a Purpose

Exercise (pages 111-112)

The thesis of the three-paragraph statement is "A common myth about the nature of mathematical ability holds that one either has or does not have a mathematical mind." The two terms in the thesis that should be circled are <u>myth</u> and <u>mathematical mind</u>. The first of the connecting lines should be drawn from <u>common myth</u> to <u>this mythology</u> in paragraph 2, line 1. Some students may continue the line to <u>the idea</u> in paragraph 3, line 4, since <u>idea</u> here means "myth." The second connecting line should be drawn from <u>mathematical mind</u> to the same expression in paragraph 1, line 8; in paragraph 2, line 2; and in paragraph 3, line 4. Some students may include <u>nonmathematical minds</u>, in paragraph 2, line 5, and <u>nonmathematical</u>, in paragraph 3, line 2.

SPECIAL PARAGRAPHS

INTRODUCTORY PARAGRAPHS

This section presents two kinds of introductory paragraph: the thesis paragraph and the "hook." The value of the first should be particularly emphasized. If the basic point of a paper is announced near the opening, the reader is able--even from the beginning of a first reading--to understand details in the context of the larger idea that is being developed. Furthermore, if the commitment comes early, the writer's awareness of the thesis will help prevent digressions from the real subject.

The strategy that determines the form of the introductory paragraph about fraternities (page 113) is worthy of emphasis, along with the "rule of thumb" that follows the paragraph. The last sentence of the introductory paragraph is an excellent place for the thesis of a paper. The writer leads into the thesis rather than stating it abruptly in the first sentence of the paper, and the position of the thesis enables the writer to move smoothly into the first topical paragraph.

You may want to talk with your students about McCrimmon's analysis of the paragraph that both states the thesis and functions as a "hook" (page 115). Few introductory paragraphs perform both of these functions, but students should know that writing such a paragraph is an option open to them.

TRANSITIONAL PARAGRAPHS

It is easy to show the function of transitional paragraphs. You may need to anticipate one problem, though. A few students who have dutifully listened to you stress the need for completeness in paragraph development may think you have suddenly reversed your field. So when you are teaching the function of the transitional paragraph you may need to explain that it can be complete <u>for its purpose</u> without the usual topic sentence and development.

Paragraphs: Units of Development   59

CONCLUDING PARAGRAPHS

At the beginning of the material on concluding paragraphs, McCrimmon stresses that not all papers need conventional concluding paragraphs. He cites two examples. You can discuss these profitably with the class, for some of your students are likely to believe that a concluding paragraph is a necessity.

After explaining that not all papers require concluding paragraphs, McCrimmon gives examples of how such paragraphs, when needed, can strengthen a paper: he presents "a paragraph that emphasizes main points in a summary," one "that draws a conclusion from preceding paragraphs," and one "that evaluates what has been done." Since many, perhaps most, student papers do need concluding paragraphs, this section of the chapter merits close attention.

A question that is almost certain to arise is this: "If the concluding paragraph tells what the paper is about, couldn't it just as well serve as an introductory paragraph? The answer, of course, is no. To make this point, ask your students to try reading the last paragraph of "Three Points of View" (pages 20-22) and the last paragraph of "You Are What You Smoke" (pages 200-201) as introductions. They will see that the writers of these paragraphs have capitalized on what they have said earlier and that the statements made in the concluding paragraphs simply are not allowable until the paragraphs out of which they grow have been presented.

Unfortunately, sometimes the concluding paragraph is used to state the point that the writer intended to make but didn't. The fact that the student did not develop the thesis convincingly may not deter him or her from beginning the last paragraph with "Therefore" or "Thus we see." Almost certainly someone in your class will need to be reminded that such a beginning for a final paragraph will not make right what has gone wrong before.

DETECTING WEAKNESSES IN PARAGRAPHS

Exercise A (pages 118-119)

This exercise requires careful work. Because it is demanding, and because the directions are structured to enable students to arrive at correct conclusions about weaknesses in paragraph structure, insist that they follow the directions closely.

1. In the first paragraph in the left column, each sentence after the topic sentence is relevant to the topic sentence.

2. The same is true of the second paragraph in the left column.

3. (In addition to the sentence numbers, the sentence itself, or an abbreviated version, is given for your convenience as you conduct the discussion.)

Left-column version

(1) Democracy is the easiest form of government because it permits all citizens a high degree of freedom.

    (2) freedom to think, talk, worship, work as people please

        (transition)

(3) (most difficult because) it makes demands on citizens

    (4) requires them to be informed about country's needs

    (5) requires them to choose among conflicting policies

    (6) demands that they distinguish between special interests and general welfare

    (7) insists that they observe both will of majority and rights of minorities

    (8) requires them to sense present and future effects of policies

4. In the first paragraph of the right column, sentences 2 and 3 should be questioned. In the second paragraph of the right column, sentences 6 and 8, and possibly 7, should be questioned. (You will notice, of course, that the second paragraph needs to be rewritten with sentence 8 as the topic sentence.) Following is a summary of the structure of the right-column paragraphs.

Right-column version

(1) Democracy is the easiest form of government because it allows people to think and speak as they please.

    (2) have to make choices between candidates

        (3) must be well informed

    (4) can engage in any occupation, join any church, or join none

(5) must do what is best for the country

    (6) have more freedom

    (7) need a good education to know what is right for them and their children

    (8) most difficult because it makes demands on citizens

    (9) must respect rights of others, obey will of majority; government must be by all of the people to be a democracy

Paragraphs: Units of Development   61

5. Obviously, the paragraphs that your students write will vary. But much of the evidence they have accumulated should lead them to speak about the need for unity in paragraphs and the relationship between unity and the coherence that grows out of a logical ordering of sentences. Some should comment on the result of the unfortunate placement of what should have been the topic sentence for the second paragraph in the right column. And, though the exercise does not ask students to consider the beneficial effect of deliberate repetition of structure and the deliberate repetition of the pronoun <u>it</u>, some may comment on these matters as they discuss the second paragraph in the left column.

<u>Exercise B</u> (page 119)

The material that follows is one writer's step-by-step response to the exercise. You may find that studying this material will be helpful as you prepare to make the writing assignment and as you conduct a prewriting discussion intended to get the students started in their note-taking. If you decide to share the short paper with the students, you should not do that, of course, until the follow-up discussion on the writing exercise.

<u>Sentence-by-sentence analysis of contrasts</u>

--No topic sentence to announce subject of paragraph.

--First sentence announces subject of paragraph. Word <u>contrast</u> is used in announcement.

--No definite association shown between sentences 1 and 2, though each speaks of a kind of art.

--Sentence 2 combines sentences 1 and 2 of the first paragraph.

--Contrast of pornography and legitimate artistic painting.

--Use of <u>just a few doors down the street</u> to show physical closeness of contrasted elements.

--Both sentences 3 and 4 speak about music, but no relationship between two sentences is apparent.

--Sentence 3 combines sentences 3 and 4 of the first paragraph.

--Shows that though sources of music are close, purposes of music are different.

--Use of <u>yet</u> and <u>not far away</u> to signal contrast and proximity.

62 Teaching with a Purpose

--Sentences 5, 6, and 7 speak of dancing girls. Though 6 and 7 are obviously related, there is no suggestion of an association between these two sentences and sentence 5.

--Sentence 4 combines sentences 5, 6, and 7 of the first paragraph in such a way that one clearly sees the contrast between those dancing girls who are inept and those who are graceful.

--Use of but to signal contrast.

--Use of word contrast.

Grouping of notes according to major types of changes

--A topic sentence has been added; it announces a contrast.

--Sentences have been combined in the revised paragraph. Three sentences (averaging thirty-five words) do the work of the seven sentences (averaging seventeen words) in the first paragraph. These new sentences announce three parts of the subject: contrasts in pictorial art, in music, and in dancing girls.

--In the first paragraph there is little obvious association between sentences discussing each part of the subject. Movement from one sentence to another is abrupt. In the sentences in the second paragraph the associations showing a series of contrasts are obvious.

--In the second paragraph specific phrases are used to explain physical proximity of the contrasted elements (just a few doors down the street and not far away); except for the somewhat vague down the street, such phrases are missing from the first paragraph. In the first paragraph nothing specifically signals a contrast, but in the second paragraph yet (sentence 3) and but (sentence 4) signal contrasts.

The Short Paper

The changes in the original paragraph about Bourbon Street have been made to point up the unity of the paragraph and to bring coherence to the paragraph so that the message will be clearer.

Actually, the first version of the paragraph has unity, but that unity is concealed. The addition of a topic sentence clearly announces the one subject of the paragraph, the "contrast of vulgarity and art" in Bourbon Street. The unity will be more obvious when the sentences, which stand as only vaguely related statements, can be made to cohere.

Coherence is established in the paragraph in two ways. One way is through the combining of sentences so that contrasted elements, the vulgar and the artistic, appear in one rather long sentence instead of in two or three shorter sentences. Thus the contrast based on pictorial art appears in one sentence, that on music in another, and that on dancing girls in a third sentence. The association of the contrasted elements is obvious here, whereas in the first paragraph the contrasted elements are in separate sentences that seem to have little relationship to each other. Coherence is also established in the second paragraph through the use of transitional words and phrases that signal contrasts and show that the contrasts exist almost side by side. <u>Just a few doors down the street</u> and <u>not far away</u> show the proximity of the contrasted elements; <u>yet</u> and <u>but</u> signal contrasts.

The changes were made, then, to create a unified and coherent paragraph that presents a series of contrasts of "vulgarity and art" on Bourbon Street.

CHAPTER 6   SENTENCES: PATTERNS OF EXPRESSION

Earlier chapters emphasize the importance of discovering what to say and how to organize the essay and the individual paragraphs. Here McCrimmon moves to a discussion of the sentence to help students develop the kinds of competence at this level that will cause the sentences to function within the larger elements with precision and in accordance with the writer's purpose.

The emphasis here is on the use of sentence patterns that express the writer's meaning most effectively, not just correctly. Most of what McCrimmon says about the grammar of the sentence is in the handbook section of the text. When grammatical terminology is used here, as it must be from time to time, the purpose is to show how grammatical structure helps the writer to say best exactly what he or she means. That is, infinitive phrases may be cited as useful in developing a sentence through modification, or noun clauses to show how two parts of a sentence are sometimes purposefully balanced on either side of the verb to be. But the focus in this chapter is on patterns that cause sentences to function well as rhetorical units.

The chapter is divided into two basic sections: a discussion of three kinds of sentences and a section on revising sentences. The kinds of sentence presented are the standard, balanced, and periodic. By far the most detailed of these subsections is that devoted to the standard sentence, for here the text presents such matters as modification, subordination, coordination, the combining of sentences, and parallel structures. You may need to remind your students that these techniques and characteristics are also applicable to the construction of the balanced sentence and the periodic sentence.

When you are talking with your students about sentences as patterns of expression, keep in mind that most of their previous instruction about sentences has been concerned with correctness in grammar and usage. Some students may have been urged to achieve variety in grammatical patterns and in sentence length in order to avoid monotony. Explain that you are after more, that you want them to be able to create particular kinds of sentence pattern in order to achieve the rhetorical effects desired.

The effect of sentence density and sentence maturity is also discussed in the first half of the chapter. You should discuss the terms density and maturity, for students are not accustomed to

Sentences: Patterns of Expression   65

seeing these words, especially density, in the context in which they are used here. (Kellogg Hunt's work, cited on page 125 in the text and in the bibliography of this manual, is the most authoritative study of the relationship between grammatical density and the maturity of a sentence.)

The second basic section of the chapter is devoted to revising sentences to achieve clarity, suitable emphasis, economy, and variety in sentence structure. The revision section is in harmony with one of the underlying principles of Writing with a Purpose, that of giving the student immediate writing experience intended to reinforce what has just been learned. The stress is always on helping the writer to know how to say exactly what he or she means, how to achieve purpose in the most effective way.

Revision is a part of the writing process with which most students have had little experience. Once the phrasing has passed from the mind to the page--too often before the writer has fully understood his or her meaning in the prewriting stage--it takes on permanent form. As Somerset Maugham says in The Summing Up, "The idea acquires substance by taking on a visible nature, and then stands in the way of its own clarification." Many of your students can correct competently mistakes that you point out, but revision is a different matter. They need instruction and practice in revision.

MODIFICATION

Exercise (page 124)

Since this exercise is open-ended, no "correct" answers can be given. But the following responses to the problems may be helpful as illustrative material.

2. By Super Bowl time professional football has become boring, because by then we have been saturated with games on week nights and weekends for more than four months.

3. Memories of the family's gathering for Mom's Sunday evening dinners make me homesick.

4. College students should be given more responsibility for determining what courses are most appropriate for the kinds of degrees they want.

5. Some people charge that beauty contests are sexist because the young women must display their physical beauty and must refrain from making statements that would mark them as hostile to the traditional view of womanhood.

6. Because my uncle has served well as a city commissioner, I am very hopeful about the outcome of his race for mayor.

7. On this campus there is a double standard for male and female students concerning check-in rules in dorms and permission to live off campus.

8. He walked toward me holding his side and staggering.

9. The CBS evening news program is the best of its kind, because Walter Cronkite's serious attitude and calm manner convince the audience that a thoroughly competent professional is reporting to them.

10. The illusion that nothing could distract our chemistry professor from the subject of his lecture was broken when a first-quarter freshman raised his hand and asked, "May I be excused, please?"

SUBORDINATION

Exercise A (pages 125-126)

Sentence combining through subordination can be effected in a number of ways, of course. The following sentences show one solution for each problem.

1. Because I had always wanted the rustic country life, we bought a sturdy old farmhouse that was a mile out of town.

    (The first sentence serves as the main clause, the second sentence becomes an adverbial clause, and the third sentence becomes an adjective clause.)

2. State University won the Valley Tournament last night in a 98-94 overtime game, in which State's Karl Winster, an all-conference player, scored 35 points.

    (The first sentence serves as the main clause; the second sentence becomes an adjective clause; the third sentence, an appositive phrase within the adjective clause; the fourth, a prepositional phrase; the fifth, an adjective within the prepositional phrase; and the sixth, an adverbial phrase.)

3. A faulty railroad signal caused an accident last night in which an express ploughed into the rear of a freight train, killing five people and injuring fifty.

    (The first sentence becomes a noun phrase used as the subject of the main clause in the new sentence; the second sentence becomes an adjective clause; the third sentence becomes a direct object and an adverbial phrase; the fourth becomes parallel participial phrases.)

Sentences: Patterns of Expression   67

COORDINATION

Exercise A (pages 126-127)

1. Tuition and the expense of living away from home keep many young people from going to college.

    (The direct object in the first sentence and the subject in the second sentence have been combined to form a compound subject; they have a common predicate.)

2. Energy consumption and inflation are two major problems in this country.

    (The two subjects have been compounded; they have a common predicate.)

3. Journalism, secondary school teaching, and the legal profession are currently overcrowded.

    (The three subjects have been compounded into a series; they have a common predicate.)

4. The camp director, our class sponsor, and a native of the area warned us against trying to shoot the rapids.

    (The three subjects have been compounded into a series; they have a common predicate.)

5. The prisoner lost 65 pounds by fasting, escaped from his cell through a small skylight, and then fled the state.

    (The three predicates have been compounded into a series; they have a common subject.)

SUBORDINATION AND COORDINATION

Exercise B (page 127)

Your students will be tempted to combine main clauses as they write new sentences. Perfectly good sentences can be written using this technique, but that practice will reduce the challenge of the exercise and will not contribute to the grammatical density of the new sentences. The writer of the following sentences has permitted himself to use more than one main clause in only one sentence, the last one.

> Last night the baseball game being played between the Minnesota Twins and the Boston Red Sox at the Twins' park was stopped in the middle of the fourth inning after an unidentified person phoned the police and reported that a bomb had been placed under the stands. The crowd was told of the report and was asked to clear the stands while the police searched for a bomb. When they found none the fans

were allowed to return to their seats, and the game was resumed after a total delay of 45 minutes.

USING PARALLEL STRUCTURES

Exercise A (page 132)

1. We hold these truths to be self-evident ── ┌ that all men are created equal,
   └ that they are endowed by their Creator with certain unalienable Rights . . . .

(Two *that* clauses forming a compound appositive, which refers to *truths*.)

2. The book is full of stories ── ┌ of sinking ships and burning towns,
   ├ of killing cold and windlashed waves, and
   └ of reckless men engaged in dangerous pursuits.

(A series of prepositional phrases. In the first two phrases there are compound objects, each part of which is modified by a verbal adjective.)

Exercise B (page 132)

1. Big cars are more powerful, more comfortable, more prestigious, and safer in a crash than small cars; but small cars are easier to park, have a lower purchase price, cost less to repair, and get better gas mileage.

2. When we watch a football game on television we see close-up details of the action, hear expert commentators' explanations of each play, see replays of particularly interesting or crucial plays, and enjoy the comfort of watching in our own homes.

Exercise C (page 132)

Advantages of watching football in the stadium

full view of each play
bands and cheering sections
excitement of the crowd
being a part of the event

When we watch a football game on television we see close-up details of the action, hear expert commentators' explanations of each play, see replays of particularly interesting or crucial plays, and enjoy the comfort of watching in our own homes; but when we watch a football game in the stadium we have a full view of each play, see and

Sentences: Patterns of Expression   69

hear the bands and cheering sections throughout the game, feel the excitement of the crowd, and enjoy the sense of being a part of the event.

REVISION FOR CLARITY

Exercise (page 138)

1. Minor revision: His sister formerly lived in Springfield, where she directed a local program that screened reports of child abuse and made referrals to case workers. She has recently moved to Washington, having been employed by the Department of Health, Education, and Welfare because of her success in Springfield.

   Major revision: Because of her success as director of a child-abuse prevention program in Springfield, his sister has been employed by the Department of Health, Education, and Welfare in Washington.

   (The original version contains 58 words in one sentence. The minor revision has 47 words in two sentences. The major revision has 29 words in one sentence. Both revisions are preferable to the original because they are clearer. Some students may assume that of the two revised versions in each of the exercise problems the major revision is preferable simply because it is shorter. You will want to be sure that such an assumption does not go uncorrected, for getting freshmen to use enough detail is a major problem. The writer should prefer one or the other of the revisions, depending on how much detail is needed to fulfill his or her purpose. This same reasoning is applicable to the revisions that follow in this exercise.)

2. Minor revision: For several years controversy has centered upon a commonly used herbicide called 2-4-5-T. Producers insist that it is not harmful to humans, but independent researchers say there is evidence that it can cause miscarriages and cancer, among other problems. The controversy has been highly publicized recently because the herbicide is similar in its chemical make-up to the defoliant used by the American military in Vietnam that is now suspected of causing cancer and other serious diseases.

   Major revision: The controversy about the harmfulness of a commonly used herbicide called 2-4-5-T has recently increased because of current charges that a defoliant used by the American military in Vietnam has caused cancer and other serious diseases. The common herbicide is similar in chemical make-up to the more potent defoliant.

   (The original version has 95 words in one sentence; the minor revision has 76 words in three sentences; the major revision has 49 words in two sentences.)

3. **Minor revision**: My father has a friend who insists that he is dirt poor. I suppose that in a sense he is, for he invests almost all of his extra income in land. He won't put his money in the bank because inflation decreases the value more than interest increases it, he doesn't want to be bothered with the problems that go along with rental property, and he isn't interested in stocks and bonds. So he buys land, reasoning that no more land is being made and that it can only continue to increase in value.

Major revision: A friend of my father invests almost all of his extra income in land. Because of inflation, he won't deposit his money in a bank, and he isn't interested in rental property or stocks and bonds. Furthermore, he is convinced that land values will continue to rise.

(The original version has 112 words in one sentence; the minor revision has 94 words in four sentences; the major revision has 47 words in three sentences.)

REVISION FOR EMPHASIS

Exercise (pages 139-140)

1. He said that, although the UN had done much of which it could be proud and was still performing valuable services in many areas, it had failed in its chief function, to preserve the peace.

2. Morality, I sometimes think, may consist chiefly in the courage of making a choice.

3. The U.S. Supreme Court's recent decision about pornography has caused much concern about censorship.

4. Our environment is threatened by an important problem to which we have only recently given much attention, noise pollution.

5. He was accused of cheating and, at a meeting of the Disciplinary Committee yesterday afternoon, he was expelled from college.

6. The governor said that, after he had considered the arguments for and against a stay of execution and had taken everything into account, he was in favor of mercy.

7. The doctor told me I could eat anything I pleased while I was on this diet, except animal fats.

8. Our traditional neglect of the men in the office of Vice President was expressed by Thomas Marshall, Vice President under Woodrow Wilson, when he said, "If you're not coming in, throw me a peanut."

Sentences: Patterns of Expression 71

9. Proposition 13, which was approved by the voters of California in 1978, served as a stimulus for a nationwide concern about reducing taxes.

10. Most political candidates, we can be sure, will promise a reduction in taxes.

11. Pete Rose hit the ball to the right field wall, but after rounding first and second and diving into third in a headfirst slide, he was called "Out!"

12. The decreased value of the dollar added to the seriousness of the situation faced by hundreds of American travelers stranded at the London airport.

REVISION FOR EMPHATIC VOICE

Exercise (page 142)

1. Once the danger was gone, we abandoned the safety precautions that we had observed so carefully.

2. Vida Blue pitched an almost perfect game.

3. The garage mechanic estimated that the repairs would cost $200.

4. Gloria Steinem spoke to a local women's club about the feminist movement.

5. Everyone in our group descended the path to the bottom of the canyon.

6. The National Rifle Association has persistently opposed gun control laws.

7. Each of our running backs scored a touchdown during the game.

8. He was not prepared for the test and so answered only half of the questions.

9. The instructor said he would grade and return the papers within three days.

10. The American Hospital Association must surely recognize that many families cannot afford such costs.

REVISION FOR ECONOMY

Exercise (page 145)

1. Often ~~the~~ his words ~~that he uses~~ do not convey ~~the~~ his meaning. ~~that he intends.~~

72 Teaching with a Purpose

2. She looked ~~as though she was feeling~~ ill.

3. ~~As far as the average citizen is concerned, it is probable that~~ M probably most people are not greatly concerned about the scandals of politicians.

4. When we studied defense mechanisms~~, which we did~~ in psychology class, I discovered that I use most of those ~~mechanisms that are~~ discussed in the textbook.

5. Just before ~~the time when~~ World War I ~~broke out~~, Alsatians ~~who were~~ of French descent were outraged by ~~the act of~~ a German soldier's slapping a cobbler ~~who was~~ (lame) across the face with a sword.

6. ~~Concerning the question of~~ Whether men are stronger than women, ~~it seems to me that the answer is variable,~~ depends on how one interprets the word stronger.

7. When~~, after much careful and painstaking study of the many and~~ space flight ~~various problems involved,~~ experts ~~in charge of the different~~ decided ~~phases of our space flight programs made the decision~~ to send a rescue ship to bring back the astronauts ~~who were in space~~ in Skylab II, about a thousand people set to work at Cape Kennedy, ~~each with his or her own duties to perform,~~ to get the rescue ship ready. ~~to fly into space and bring back the astronauts.~~

REVISION FOR VARIETY

Exercise (pages 147-148)

1. Shakespeare's chronicle history of Henry the Fifth, a drama of kinghood and war, is essentially a play about a young king's coming of age.

2. Henry V, who had been an irresponsible young prince before his accession to the throne, had to prove his worthiness as king by leading his army in war.

3. and 4. After invading France and capturing Harfleur, he tried to withdraw his troops to Calais; but he and his men were confronted by a numerically superior French army at Agincourt.

5. In a famous passage in Shakespeare's play, Henry urges his soldiers on to an incredible victory, in which the superior mobility and firepower of the English proved too much for the heavily armored French.

Review Exercise A (pages 148-149)

The basic problem in the paragraph on lobbyists is the lack of variety in the sentences. This has been corrected in the version below. Following the revised paragraph is an explanation of the changes that have been made.

> The most successful lobbyists working in state capitols are highly paid experts in legislative strategy, who know more about the legislative process than do most state legislators. They are skillful, professional workers, available to almost any group with sufficient funds to pay for their services. Today lobbyists are not likely to apply the old-fashioned direct pressure to politicians; instead they are likely to try to persuade legislators' constituents to apply the pressure. In this way they hope to convince legislators that what the pressure group wants is what the public wants.

Sentences 1, 2, and 3 have been combined. 2 has been converted into an adjective phrase and 3 into an adjective clause.

Sentences 4 and 5 have been combined. 5 has been converted into an adjective phrase.

Sentences 6 and 7 have been combined. _Today_ in 6 has been moved to the beginning of the new sentence to break the monotony of opening sentences with subjects and to emphasize _today_. _Instead_ has been written between 6 and 7 to provide transition.

Sentences 8 and 9 have been combined. The independent clauses of 8 have become noun clauses in the new sentence. _In this way_ provides transition into the new sentence.

Review Exercise B (page 149)

The problem in the following paragraph is wordiness. This can be corrected by crossing out a number of words and by doing some rephrasing. The original version contains 166 words; the revised version, 99.

One of the misconceptions that many people have about language is that it will "hold still" and refuse to change. And many who know that our English language has continuously changed through the years suspect that there is something bad about this change. You may have heard someone regret that our language is no longer the "grand old language of Shakespeare." That person would be surprised to learn that Shakespeare was one of those denounced for corrupting the English language. But change in our language is not to be deplored: it is simply a fact that we must accept.

CHAPTER 7   DICTION: THE CHOICE OF WORDS

The chapter on diction comes at the end of this sequence: focus on (1) the whole paper (in four prewriting chapters), (2) paragraphs, (3) sentences, and (4) words and phrases in the sentence. And it serves as preparation for the chapter on style, which follows immediately.

After McCrimmon discusses briefly how words express their meaning through denotation and connotation, he organizes his chapter around two main headings:

Three Qualities of Good Diction

>   --appropriateness, specificity, and imagery

>   and

Revising Diction

>   --to remove vagueness, jargon, triteness and ineffective imagery

This organization is in harmony with one of the basic teaching strategies in the text: (1) giving the student the information needed in the prewriting and writing stages and then (2) asking him or her to examine writing critically and to improve it through rewriting.

APPROPRIATENESS

Questions about what diction is appropriate and what is not arise time after time in writing classes. Students continually confronted with the marginal notation D and no other explanation may become genuinely confused and wonder what mysterious standard determines what they can and cannot appropriately say. And new teachers are often puzzled about what to tell their students. The position on appropriateness taken in Writing with a Purpose is that "words are appropriate when they are suited to the writer's purpose, which includes the writer's analysis of the situation and of the audience for which the writing is intended" (page 153).

One way to help students teach themselves the importance of the situation and of the relationship between the writer and the reader is to ask them to write short explanations giving the same information to two different audiences. For example, a student might write to the college academic-probation committee and to a friend in another school a brief explanation of his or her low grade-point average last term and of plans to correct the situation. The committee might read such phrases as "numerous social activities" and "resolution to bring discipline to my work habits," but the friend might read "too many parties" and "determination to stay at the books." Several pairs of these paragraphs can serve as the basis for a class discussion on how a piece of writing is influenced by the situation and by the relationship between the writer and the reader.

Your students may never have considered consciously the influence of subject matter on diction. The following example can help you make the point. A small-town weekly newspaper used this sentence in a front-page news story: "One of the most sensational auto wrecks that this community has known in years netted six lives last Saturday." Most of your students will see immediately that the subject matter makes inappropriate the words <u>sensational</u>, <u>auto</u>, <u>wrecks</u>, and <u>netted</u>. <u>Automobile</u> and <u>accident</u>, replacing <u>auto</u> and <u>wreck</u>, will help to establish the tone the news writer should want. But <u>sensational</u> and <u>netted</u> are the chief offenders: the first suggests something thrilling, and the second suggests something gained.

Once your students have learned about the elements of a rhetorical situation that influence diction, they may still need to be reminded of the need for consistency in diction. A student may examine with considerable formality the possibility of eliminating the office of Vice President of the United States and then conclude, "Most of the evidence suggests that the American people are <u>stuck</u> with the Vice Presidency." Again, the damage that results from inconsistent diction can be seen in the concluding paragraph of a student's paper about her former employer, named Leroy:

> Leroy must have had some redeeming qualities. We never troubled to find them. ~~But there seemed to be missing from his being the vibrancy, the élan vital necessary to stimulate a relationship.~~ We didn't like Leroy.

Once the next-to-the-last sentence is removed, the diction is appropriately consistent with the informal language of the rest of the paper.

One matter related to consistency in diction that can be troublesome for beginning teachers is the use of the term <u>slang</u> in the marking of papers. Some teachers seem to classify as slang a great many words of which they disapprove. If a word is excessively informal for the context in which the student has used it, the diction is inconsistent, and the teacher should point out the problem. But when the instructor arbitrarily and abruptly excludes a word with only the comment "Slang," the student can become puzzled and resentful. Help is readily available for the instructor who is determined to use the term with discretion, for <u>slang</u> is employed as a usage label in some of the better desk dictionaries (<u>American Heritage</u>,

Diction: The Choice of Words   77

Webster's New Collegiate, Webster's New World). If none of these dictionaries labels a word as slang, the instructor should refrain from declaring it to be that.

Discussion Problem A (page 158)

The speaker is apparently both an imaginative and an unschooled man. The occasion was a crucial one for him, for his trial was almost over and within a few minutes the jury would begin to determine whether he was innocent or guilty of murder. The naturalness of his language, the simplicity of the metaphor (particularly striking because he sees his accusers rather than himself as the trapped), and the urgency of the voice we hear are all in harmony with each other.

Discussion Problem B (page 158)

In the version of the paragraph below, the excessively informal diction has been replaced by more appropriate terms.

One serious ~~rap~~ *charge* that has been made against pressure groups is that they wield power without corresponding responsibility. Because they do not have to stand the test of power by winning elections, they are able to make ~~beefed-up~~ *exaggerated* claims about the ~~clout~~ *influence* the people they represent give them. If these claims are made confidently, timid members of Congress are likely to be impressed. Some people think that this susceptibility of politicians to being ~~hoodwinked~~ *deceived* is increased by the failure of the great political parties to support their members against the pressure groups. Others feel that Congress itself is too ~~wishy-washy-about~~ *lenient toward* propagandists. Whatever the cause, the irresponsibility of pressure groups has fostered ~~ripoffs~~ *abuses* that distort their legitimate function to ~~tip-off~~ *advise* legislators concerning public policy.

SPECIFICITY

Exercise (page 160)

1. athlete, football player, quarterback, Roger Staubach

2. animal, quadruped, dog, bird dog, Labrador retriever

3. TV newsman, member of CBS news staff, anchor man, Walter Cronkite

4. politician, legislator, senator, Senator Edward Kennedy

5. vacation spot, West Indies, U.S. Virgin Islands, St. John Island

6. plant, bush, decorative bush, rosebush, Tropicana rosebush

7. criminal, thief, pickpocket, the man who stole my wallet

Comments on specificity, generality, concreteness, and abstractness

Teachers and students sometimes carelessly assume when discussing diction that <u>specific</u> and <u>concrete</u> have the same meaning and that <u>general</u> and <u>abstract</u> are synonymous. The terms are used with more precision in this chapter than these assumptions would permit.

To help your students understand the distinctions, you can ask them to construct a specific-to-general ladder, using as data their answers to one of the problems in the exercise on page 160. For example:

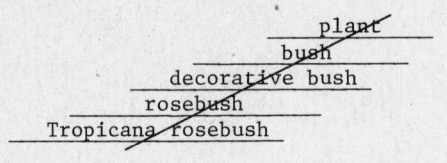

```
                    plant
                  bush
              decorative bush
            rosebush
        Tropicana rosebush
```

In relation to other items on this ladder, <u>plant</u> is the most general, but we would not say that it is an abstract term. It and the other items down through the most specific, <u>Tropicana rosebush</u>, are likely to be classified as concrete items.

After discussing the ladder above, you can ask your students to consider the following one.

```
                    theorem
                mathematics theorem
              geometry theorem
           Euclidean geometry theorem
       Pythagorean theorem (a² + b² = c²)
```

<u>Theorem</u> suggests both generality and abstractness. But, though the term <u>Pythagorean theorem</u> suggests specificity, the concept that it represents is abstract, not concrete.

All this is not to suggest that there is no relationship between specificity and concreteness and between generality and abstractness. Instead, the point is that the assumption that each set of terms is a pair of synonyms is erroneous and can lead to confusion in the classroom.

Diction: The Choice of Words   79

Exercise A (page 162)

The following phrases are striking for their specificity and concreteness: green crawling scum, blue gulps, sparkling like liquid sky, quivered in a jug, and work your mouth like a fish. These expressions clearly show that the passage grew out of the writer's close observation of the scene.

Exercise B (pages 162-163)

In the paragraphs about swimming, the more concrete diction is in the paragraph in the right-hand column. A comparison of the following phrases will make the point.

| some neighboring stream | the crick below the pasture |
| some discarded article of clothing | her brother's outgrown overalls |

In the paragraphs about the snake the more concrete diction is in the paragraph in the left-hand column.

the biceps of my right arm	my arm
(detailed description of the snake's movement and of how the movement felt to the person)	I felt the snake moving
	I felt the contraction of its muscles
a flat, V-shaped head, with two glistening, black protruding buttons	its ugly head and its evil-looking eyes
A thin, pointed, sickening yellow tongue slipped out, then in	its tongue kept moving in and out
a sound like that of escaping steam	a kind of hissing noise

Exercise C (page 163)

You should emphasize that it is advisable for the student to write from experience in this exercise. The scene or incident described should be real, or at least based on reality; for the writer is asked to be as specific and concrete as possible. The student who relies on imagination may speak in terms that tend toward abstractness and generality.

A first-quarter freshman once taught her teacher the value of this sort of writing exercise. New at the university, she was determined to give the teacher the kind of writing she was sure a college professor of English would want. The vague diction and convoluted sentence structure made her paper as nearly unintelligible as any the instructor had ever read by a normally bright student.

In fact, he feared that the problem was so severe that remediation more specialized than he was competent to direct might be necessary.

In the follow-up conference the instructor asked the student to recall some incident that meant a great deal to her at the time it occurred and whose details were still vivid in her mind. She said that when she was about five years old and giving her first dance recital she fell flat on her face and lay on the stage too embarrassed to move. The teacher told the student that he would leave the office for a few minutes and that she should write the details of the incident just as they had happened. She did--in perfectly clear, concrete, straightforward prose. When the instructor praised what she had written, the young woman said, "Why, I didn't think an English professor would want anything simple like that." The serious problem that the instructor had feared simply did not exist; the student just needed to begin to learn some elementary principles of clear writing, especially the value of being specific.

IMAGERY

When you are talking with students about how similes and metaphors work, you can explain that the comparisons made are of things so dissimilar that they belong to different classes. You can illustrate this point by working with illustrations from the text. For example:

1. Change Steinbeck's "She crouched like a fawning dog" (page 164) to "She crouched like a person who was terribly afraid." The simile disappears.

2. Change Jane Howard's "Good families are fortresses" (page 166) to "Good families are social units . . . ." The metaphor is gone.

One of the problems that students have when they are learning to use imagery in their writing is their occasional loss of control of the image. This problem becomes particularly troublesome when the student is trying to work out an extended analogy. The analogy, like the simile and the metaphor, compares things that are essentially dissimilar (see the Gregory excerpt, pages 166-167, in which a hardened soul and a callused foot are the bases for the analogy). But once the essential difference has been granted, the reader must be able to see that designated parts of the two things function similarly. If the comparisons of parts conspicuously fail this test, the image is lost.

The paragraph that follows illustrates this problem. In case you want to use the material for class discussion, an analysis of the problem accompanies the paragraph. (Do not rely on an oral reading of the analogy. The problems are sufficiently complex for students to need to see the paragraph on the board or in dittoed form.)

One precautionary note. An instructor should be gentle while criticizing such writing, lest the student decide that it is best to abandon the use of analogies and images. If the young woman who wrote this paragraph can learn to control her figurative language, she will become a better writer.

> (1) The basic purpose of the two-year college should be to enable students to develop their capabilities. (2) The junior college should provide for students the proper climate in which to grow; their abilities must have a background from which to emerge. (3) The rich soil from which students must develop ought to contain knowledge of their environment and the skills they will need to cope with their surroundings. (4) Reasoning ability is an important ingredient in the mixture, serving as fertilizer to add to its fruitfulness. (5) From this concrete foundation should climb a vine with various stems, all culminating in the blossoming of the students' potential resources.

Analysis of the paragraph

The analogy depends upon a comparison of (1) the students' developing within the junior college environment and (2) a plant's developing within its environment. So the student and the plant are analogous.

Sentence 2   The problem of determining the other parts of the analogy begins in this sentence and increases as the paragraph continues. Vines grow in climate; students grow in the environment of the junior college. What the background is in each of the parts of the analogy is uncertain. And there is a minor problem in finding something in the vine part of the analogy to correlate with the students' abilities.

Sentence 3   Vines grow from rich soil; students develop from knowledge and skills. The problem arises when we try to compare the way in which the rich soil contains a knowledge of the vine's environment with the way in which students' knowledge and skills contain a knowledge of the students' environment. Both parts of the analogy lack precision; the analogy is at best vague.

Sentence 4   We can see that the soil is enriched by fertilizer and that in a sense the students' knowledge and skills are enriched by their reasoning ability. We can grant, too, that the fertilizer contributes to the fruitfulness of the soil (or at least of the vine) and that reasoning ability contributes to the fruitfulness of knowledge and skills (or at least of the students). But does the soil have or develop fertilizer in the way that students have or develop reasoning ability? (We may be looking too closely at the analogy here; we could overlook this sort of inconsistency if the rest of the analogy held together.)

Sentence 5   The writer is no doubt accustomed to thinking of the desirability of a firm foundation--the kind a building should have.

82   Teaching with a Purpose

But should the foundation that a vine grows from have the sort of firmness suggested by <u>concrete</u>?

<u>Sentence 5</u> Finally there is the blossoming. We might (tolerantly) accept the blossoming of students' resources if we were not entangled in the vine analogy. But when we are asked to visualize the blossoming of the vine's resources, we are faced with the necessity of seeing blossoms on roots.

<u>Exercise A</u> (pages 168-169)

In the paragraphs below, the underscored words are some of those that give the paragraphs their specificity and imagery. Students' responses will vary from those given here, of course.

When the wild ducks or the wild geese migrate in their season, <u>a strange tide rises</u> in the territories over which they <u>sweep</u>. As if <u>magnetized</u> by the <u>great triangular flight</u>, the barnyard fowl leap a foot or two into the air and try to fly, . . . and <u>a vestige of savagery quickens their blood</u>. All the ducks on the farm are transformed for an instant into migrant birds, and into <u>those hard little heads</u>, till now filled with humble <u>images of pools and worms and barnyards</u>, there <u>swims a sense of continental expanse</u>, of the <u>breadth of seas</u> and the <u>salt taste of the ocean wind</u>. The duck <u>totters</u> to the right and left in its wire enclosure, <u>gripped</u> by a sudden passion to perform the impossible and a sudden love whose object is a mystery.

The word is terracide. As in homicide, or genocide. Except it's terra. Land.

It is not committed with guns and knives, but with <u>great, relentless bulldozers</u> and <u>thundering dump trucks</u>, with <u>giant shovels like mythological creatures</u>, their <u>girdered necks lifting massive steel mouths</u> high above the tallest trees. And with dynamite. <u>They cut and blast and rip apart mountains</u> to reach the minerals inside, and when they have finished there is nothing left but <u>naked hills, ugly monuments to waste, stripped</u> of everything that once held them in place, cut off from the top and sides and dug out from the inside and then left, <u>restless</u>, to <u>slide down on houses</u> and wash off into rivers and streams, rendering the land unlivable and the water for miles downstream undrinkable.

Terracide. Or, if you prefer, strip-mining.

Smoke was rising here and there among the creepers that <u>festooned</u> the dead or dying trees. As they watched, <u>a flash of fire appeared at the root of one wisp</u>, and then the smoke thickened. <u>Small flames stirred</u> at the trunk of a tree and <u>crawled away</u> through leaves and brushwood, <u>dividing</u> and increasing. One patch touched a tree trunk and <u>scrambled up like a bright squirrel</u>. The smoke increased, <u>sifted</u>, rolled outwards. <u>The squirrel leapt on the wings</u>

Diction: The Choice of Words   83

of the wind and clung to another standing tree, eating downwards. Beneath the dark canopy of leaves and smoke the fire laid hold on the forest and began to gnaw. Acres of black and yellow smoke rolled steadily toward the sea. At the sight of the flames and the irresistible course of the fire, the boys broke into shrill, excited cheering. The flames, as though they were a kind of wild life, crept as a jaguar creeps on its belly toward a line of birch-like saplings that fledged an outcrop of the pink rock. They flapped at the first of the trees, and the branches grew a brief foliage of fire. The heart of flame leapt nimbly across the gap between the trees and then went swinging and flaring along the whole row of them. Beneath the capering boys a quarter of a mile square of forest was savage with smoke and flame. The separate noises of the fire merged into a drum-roll that seemed to shake the mountain.

Exercise B (page 169)

Of the two versions of the paragraph, the one in the left column contains sharper images and more specific diction. In this version the stove is potbellied, and it burns wood. The customers know each other: they are regular customers. It is beer they are drinking and gossip they are talking. The light in the room is uneven, for the light bulbs are suspended from the ceiling and so sway in the draft each time the door is opened. The swaying bulbs cause the shadows to swing around the walls in an eerie fashion.

REVISING DICTION

ELIMINATING VAGUENESS

Exercise (page 171)

In the following versions of the sentences more specific terms (underscored) have been substituted for the vague expressions.

1. He is a doctor, but I don't know what his specialty is.

2. Our sorority is opposed to Brenda Ames for student president.

3. It was a successful party: congenial people, delicious food, and lively conversation.

4. What a pleasant surprise to meet so many well-informed people at the same committee meeting.

5. The actors gave a performance that won praise from critics.

6. The judge said the request was unusual but she would take it under advisement.

7. Mother is complaining about Jean's moving into her own apartment; she is really angry about it.

8. One advantage of the agreement is its effect on prices.

84   Teaching with a Purpose

9. I thought that the new TV series was <u>witty</u>, but it got <u>very</u> low ratings.

10. The price they are charging for steak is <u>too high for us to pay</u>.

<u>Exercise</u> (pages 171-172)

The more specific of each of the pairs of expressions appears (underscored) in the following version of the paragraph.

The whole surface of the ice was <u>a chaos</u> of movement. It looked like an enormous <u>jigsaw puzzle</u> stretching away to infinity and being <u>crunched</u> together by some invisible but irresistible force. The impression of its <u>titanic</u> power was heightened by the unhurried deliberateness of the motion. Whenever two thick <u>floes</u> came together, their edges <u>butted</u> and <u>ground</u> against one another for a time. Then, when neither of them showed signs of yielding, they rose <u>quiveringly</u>, driven by the <u>implacable</u> power behind them. Sometimes they would stop <u>abruptly</u> as the unseen forces affecting the ice appeared mysteriously to lose interest. More frequently, though, the two floes--often ten feet thick or more--would continue to rise, <u>tenting up</u> until one or both of them toppled over, creating a pressure ridge.

ELIMINATING JARGON

<u>Exercise</u> (page 175)

Sentence 1 can be read, <u>A fellow I worked with let me read his copy of Big Arms</u>, by Bob Hoffman.

In sentence 2 the introductory phrase is unnecessary. All that is needed is <u>I was surprised at how the book held my interest</u>.

Sentence 3 can be eliminated if <u>continued to hold</u> is substituted for <u>held</u> in sentence 2.

Sentence 4 can be read <u>After reading it, I bought a weightlifting set and exercised whenever I had a few spare minutes</u>.

The paragraph now reads:

A fellow I worked with let me read his copy of <u>Big Arms</u>, by Bob Hoffman. I was surprised at how the book continued to hold my interest. After reading it, I bought a weightlifting set and exercised whenever I had a few spare minutes.

Diction: The Choice of Words   85

ELIMINATING TRITENESS

Discussion Problem and Exercise (page 177)

We do not, of course, gain from the paragraph any new insights about the value of football. The sentiments expressed depend heavily on clichés that we have so often heard in celebration of the value of football (this is not to say that the sentiments are entirely devoid of merit). We cannot with assurance establish a cause-and-effect relationship between the triteness of the content and that of the diction, but we can suspect that there is one.

The trite diction has been replaced in the paragraph below. The revised version has 175 words; the original, 244.

Wherever ~~the gridiron game~~ football is played in the United States--on a sandlot, a high school field, or in a college or professional stadium--the players learn ~~through the school of hard knocks~~ the invaluable lesson that only by the cooperation of each man ~~men's blending together like birds of a feather~~ can the team win. It is a lesson they do not forget on the ~~gridiron~~ field. Off the field, they duly remember it. In society, the former player does not look upon himself as a ~~lone wolf on the prowl~~ loner who has the right ~~to do his own thing--that is,~~ to observe only his individual social laws. He knows he is a ~~part~~ member of society ~~of the big picture~~ and must conduct himself as such. He realizes that only by ~~playing as a team man~~ cooperating can he do his share in making society what it should be--the protector and benefactor of all. The man who has ~~been willing to make the sacrifice to play~~ played football knows that teamwork is essential in ~~this~~ modern ~~day and age~~ living and that every citizen must ~~pull his weight in the boat~~ do his part if the nation is to prosper. So he has little difficulty in adjusting to his roles in family/life ~~and in the world of business and to his duties as a citizen in the total scheme of things~~ and business. In short, his football training helps make him a better citizen and person~~, better able to play the big game of life~~.

ELIMINATING INEFFECTIVE IMAGERY

<u>Exercise</u> (pages 178-179)

1. Students surged into the corridor.

2. You have been selected for this program so that we can increase the competency of the best people that we have.

3. The defense attorney said he believed the facts would be revealed during the trial.

4. The President's ill-advised action has thrown the nation for a loss; and unless members of Congress ignore party lines and carry the ball as a team, it may take months to get the country back into its game plan.

   <u>or, much better,</u>

   The President's ill-advised action has damaged the nation; and unless members of Congress can ignore party lines and work together, it may take months for the country to overcome the effects of the damage.

5. Some of the things that policeman said would make your hair stand on end.

   <u>or</u>

   . . . would make your flesh crawl.

   <u>or</u>

   . . . would startle you.

CHAPTER 8   TONE AND STYLE

So far, Part II has discussed writing and rewriting, moving in emphasis from the paragraph to the sentence to words and phrases in the sentence. Now the book returns to matters that concern the whole paper, to the general problem of style, which includes prewriting, writing, and rewriting. This chapter draws on all that has gone before and thus offers a constructive summary of the composition process.

The chapter is divided into three main sections: "Tone," "Style," and "Some Practical Advice About Style." Tone and style, of course, cannot be separated, since tone is a part of style. But in this edition McCrimmon has chosen to deal with the writer's attitude toward the subject and reader before taking up the linguistic choices that both determine and reveal the style of a piece of writing. The practical advice at the end of the chapter provides a checklist that a student can keep in mind in writing and rewriting a first draft.

TONE

INFORMATIVE AND EFFECTIVE TONE, DISTANCE

Once students understand the technical vocabulary of the section on tone, the material should be easy for them to master. But they can have difficulty if they have not paid close attention to definitions. Probably they have never before had occasion to consider exactly what tone means to the writer. Emphasize that tone, as it will be considered here, reveals the author's attitudes about two elements of the writing situation: (1) the subject and (2) the readers. Many, perhaps most, of your students have not previously seen the terms informative, affective, and distance applied to tone. These terms should be taken up in class discussion after the students have read this section of the text. The clarifying that you do at this point will prove helpful later in the chapter when the students consider several characteristics of language that form the style of a piece of writing.

Discussion Problem (pages 185-186)

As the directions point out, the mere rating of these passages as informative or affective is less important than the identification of the evidence on which the ratings are made. The question most worth discussing is not "How are the passages to be rated?" but "Why do you rate these passages as you do?"

The Lorraine Hansberry passage is clearly the most affective of the three. This is not to say that Miss Hansberry presents no information; she does. But the informative function of the passage is subordinate to the writer's purposes: to express her emotional reaction to what she has experienced and to lead her readers to share her reactions. She uses highly affective terms: <u>lynching</u>, <u>victim of physical attack</u>, <u>racial and political hysteria</u>, <u>ravages of congenital diseases</u>, <u>afflicted with drug addiction and alcoholism and mental illness</u>, <u>greed and malice</u>, <u>indifference to human misery</u>, <u>ignorance</u>, <u>feeling heart</u>, and <u>miseries which afflict this world</u>. In the middle of the first paragraph the author moves very close to her readers by suggesting that she, "like all of you," has witnessed man's cruelty to his fellows.

Both of the other passages are more informative, and students may disagree on which one should be rated at the informative end of the scale. That decision should depend on the answer to this question: "Is the author using the information primarily to support his own attitude toward the subject, or is he simply presenting the information for its own sake?"

The Conner paragraph is a report. It describes the situation in the church without making any judgment about it. The humor of the situation will affect the reader mildly, but that humor comes from the situation, not from the author's treatment of it. His personality, feelings, or attitudes toward the scene he is describing are not introduced into his writing. He is simply "telling it as it was," not as he felt about it. This objectivity makes the paragraph an informative report.

The paragraph by E. B. White is full of information, but the author is not writing an objective report of New York; he is selecting evidence to support a judgment that reveals his attitude toward the city: it is an implausible miracle that should have destroyed itself long ago. The author wants the reader to share this subjective view of the city.

This contrast of the Conner and White passages suggests that while both contain information, White's description of the scene is the more affective. If so, it should be placed between the Conner and the Hansberry passages in the informative-affective scale.

STYLE

STYLE DEFINED and LANGUAGE

Style is a difficult subject to discuss in the classroom, partly because it is often seen primarily as an abstract concept. Aware of this difficulty, McCrimmon is careful to define <u>style</u> as he will use the term, "the pattern of choices a writer makes in

Tone and Style   89

developing his or her purpose," and to discuss thoroughly the specific elements of tone and language that form style patterns. He concentrates on particulars and reminds the student that "we are not dealing with some vague literary quality." He demonstrates the usefulness of the information he has just presented by using it to analyze and summarize the styles of three passages.

Now the author is ready to present a style scale that ranges from _formal_ through _moderate_ to _colloquial_, to explain that each of these styles "is appropriate in some situation," and to recommend that "the most appropriate style for most freshman compositions is the moderate style." (The term _moderate style_ is new in this edition, replacing _informal style_. Professor McCrimmon made the change because some teachers are reluctant to recommend a style called "informal" to their freshmen. The cause for this reluctance is that they have been taught in the schools that there are _two_ styles, formal and informal, and that student papers should be written in a formal style; therefore they associate the term _informal_ with a style they were warned against--the style that McCrimmon labels _colloquial_.)

Having described these three styles and explained the style continuum, so that the moderate blends with the formal on one side and with the colloquial on the other, McCrimmon can now present the summarizing table on page 194. This table will repay careful study by the teacher. It gives in succinct form specific characteristics of the moderate style in which most freshman papers should be written, and it identifies the formal and colloquial characteristics into which the moderate style blends. Once the teacher can make accurate statements about what a student should do about style, he or she need not rely on simplistic and inaccurate negative advice such as "Don't write a contraction," "Don't use _I_ or _we_ or _you_," "Don't . . . "--the list goes on. And there is no need to say, "Write in a formal style." The teacher should be pleased to know that there is a moderate position, with identifiable characteristics, between a very formal and a very colloquial style.

Exercise (pages 195-196)

The easiest way to discuss this exercise in class is to begin by asking, "Which is the most colloquial?" and then, "Which is the most formal?" That way the extremes of the range can make it easier to show that the first paragraph has a style intermediate between formal and colloquial.

The Churchill paragraph is by far the most formal. Its nine sentences contain over 300 words and average 34. The final sentence, with the repetitive series of main clauses ("We shall fight . . . , we shall fight . . . , we shall fight . . . ; we shall never surrender . . . ") is a conspicuous example of parallel structure, and the sentence beginning "Even though large tracts of Europe" is a periodic sentence. The distance between writer and reader (originally speaker and hearer, since the passage occurred in a speech made to British members of Parliament) is much greater than in either of the other two paragraphs; and the whole tone is, as it was meant to be, eloquent and inspiring, a dedication of the British nation to continue the war after the defeat at Dunkirk.

In the second example, both the diction and the sentence fragments clearly mark the style as colloquial. The sentences contain from 5 to 29 words, an average of 13 words per sentence. Except for the first and last sentences, the paragraph is a series of fragments with such obviously colloquial terms as _kids_, _lowdown_, _jocks_, and _john_. The distance between writer and reader is much closer than in either of the other two paragraphs.

Boulding's paragraph on the image is neither colloquial nor formal but has a moderate style that lies well within both extremes. Its fourteen sentences contain slightly more than 200 words and average 15. None of the sentences is a fragment. There are several examples of parallel structures, but none so conspicuous as the last sentence of the Churchill paragraph. With the exceptions of _implication_ and _validity_, there are no learned words, and there are no colloquialisms. The writer addresses his readers as "you," but the distance between writer and reader is not so close as in the second passage nor so remote as in the third. Clearly the style of the Boulding paragraph is intermediate between the other two.

SOME PRACTICAL ADVICE ABOUT STYLE (pages 196-199)

This section is one of fundamental importance. Its position-- near the end of a chapter that draws on the first six chapters-- marks it as such. And the author, who is not inclined toward overstatement, tells the student that this section "will give the gist of the last six chapters" and that "it will give you, in compact form, the chief considerations you have to keep in mind in all your writing." Appropriately, the seven points begin with emphasis on knowing one's purpose and letting that purpose govern decisions about style. The point is so important that all that is said "on the other six points is implied in this first one."

The fourth of the seven points is "Try to see your writing as your reader will see it"; the author acknowledges that "of all the advice given here, this is the hardest to follow." And it is. Teachers sometimes suggest that a student who is having trouble with clarity ask a friend whose judgment can be trusted and who will be candid to read the paper and place a check mark in the margin by any sentence that is not clear. Then the writer can rework those particular sentences. Another way the instructor can help students see their writing from the reader's perspective is to arrange for small-group sessions in which the students offer critiques of each other's work before the papers are submitted to the instructor. In these sessions the writer cannot avoid knowing how at least two or three readers react to the paper. Some teachers have found these small-group critique sessions most valuable; others have not. Their value seems to vary with (1) how well the instructor has prepared the students for the session, (2) how serious the students are about wanting to write well, and (3) how competent they are to offer good advice.

The author's sixth point is "Avoid wordiness." One reason this advice is difficult to follow is that writers usually do not know when they are being wordy. An excerpt from a letter from Thomas Wolfe to one of his publisher's readers will illustrate the problem. Wolfe was writing about his unusually verbose manuscript when he said, "Generally, I do not believe the writing to be wordy, prolix, or redundant." One professor, to make his students sensitive to wordiness, gives an assignment that tempts them to write seven hundred to a thousand words; but, without specifying an absolute maximum length, he asks them to assume that they will be paid five cents per word up to four hundred words and penalized ten cents for every word beyond that. Of course he is careful to choose an assignment that can be fulfilled without a sacrifice in essential content.

The last of the seven points is "Revise and proofread." You will need to continue to stress that proofreading and revision are not the same; unless you do, many of your students will think they are revising when they are merely correcting errors. But the value of proofreading for errors should not be underestimated. One professor impressed a class with the necessity for proofreading by telling his students that he was interested only in what they had to say and that he paid no attention to errors in spelling, typing, form of documentation, and grammatical usage. When a number of the students started to relax and smile, thinking they had found their kind of professor, he added, "Unless these errors distract me from what you're saying." This was his way of alerting his students that he would be the most easily distracted reader imaginable. One can regret the touch of sadism in the method without questioning the soundness of the point. It is important to make students see that the writer has a great advantage if the reader is able to concentrate on what is being said without being distracted by mistakes in elementary composition skills.

Review Exercise (pages 199-201)

The answers to these questions should prepare students to make a general statement about the style of the paper.

1. The writer's attitude toward her subject is light, subjective, and affective. She is clearly interested in making fun of cigarette advertising, and that purpose rules out an impersonal, objective, and informative approach to her subject. In general, the tone of the opening paragraph is maintained consistently throughout the paper.

2. The paper suggests that it is written for people who will respond favorably to a humorous debunking of cigarette advertising, probably people like her classmates. The distance between writer and reader is close, not the kind of over-the-shoulder closeness that you saw in the advice about painting

on page 190, but close enough so that she sometimes seems to be speaking _for_ her readers as well as _to_ them.

3. There is nothing in the paper that would allow us to classify the style as formal. The question is likely to be, "Is it moderate or colloquial?" It does have some colloquial elements: some fragments ("Nobody, right?" "Nobody but nobody," "Apparently not," "An interested person, that's who") and occasional colloquial diction ("I'll bet you a Cricket lighter"). Yet on the whole, the sentences are complete, and the vocabulary is neither learned nor colloquial but popular. The style can best be described as "moderate, with colloquial touches."

4. The class will probably agree that the style is appropriate to the purpose. It would not be appropriate in a serious criticism of cigarette advertising, but it is appropriate to this kind of criticism.

5. This is a judgment for the class to make. The fact that the paper was graded A by the student's instructor (the students do not know this, of course) indicates that appreciation of the paper is not limited to freshmen.

CHAPTER 9   PERSUASION

The chapter on persuasion comes at the end of the basic text. This position is appropriate, for the writer of a persuasive paper must rely heavily on many of the writing competencies that have been discussed earlier. It is particularly appropriate that the persuasion chapter should follow immediately the discussion of style: the writer who would persuade must be especially sensitive to what style can do toward moving an audience to accept a paper's thesis.

Early in the chapter McCrimmon explains that the kind of persuasion the chapter speaks of is a voluntary change in judgment, and the first few pages offer practical advice on how to encourage others to change their minds. The writer must have a complete understanding of the rhetorical situation: What is the relationship between the writer and the reader? What does the reader know about the subject? Is the reader's belief about, or image of, the subject shallow or deep rooted? What is the effect of the occasion? What purpose leads this writer to address this reader about this subject on this occasion? Some teachers encourage students to have in clear view as they write half a sheet of paper or a card on which is written the thesis, the persona of the writer, the reader for whom the paper is intended, the occasion, and the purpose.

Students sometimes misjudge what kind of audience they should address. Obviously there is no need to persuade someone who already agrees with the writer and no point in trying to persuade someone who refuses to consider an argument. Students should attempt to persuade people who are either uncommitted or mildly hostile toward the thesis to be argued. Though this point seems obvious, many students do not understand it. It is so basic to a successful paper that it deserves emphasis.

MEANS OF PERSUASION

The means of persuasion dealt with in the chapter are (1) trustworthiness, (2) emotional appeal, and (3) the logic of argument. McCrimmon emphasizes that, though these three means must be presented individually in the text, they are interrelated in a paper. As you teach this chapter, take advantage of every opportunity to demonstrate how these means of persuasion complement each other.

94 Teaching with a Purpose

TRUSTWORTHINESS

One way to persuade is to be trustworthy. The audience should <u>want</u> to believe and agree with the writer. To merit this trust, the writer must be knowledgeable about the subject and fair in his treatment of opposing arguments.

Writers sometimes fail to win trust because they do not consider their writing important enough to merit the effort to express their message well. You will sometimes discover in a conference about a paper that a student knew that he or she should have supported a generalization with evidence or that he or she was twisting facts to force a meaning. One way to encourage students to be trustworthy is to insist that they write on subjects they believe are significant enough to deserve their best effort. Another way is to show them that their essays will always receive careful consideration from you and, whenever possible, from part or all of the class.

<u>Exercise</u> (page 212)

Only those readers who share Mencken's extreme contempt for Bryan are likely not to find this attack objectionable. His dislike of Bryan is so completely subjective that his trustworthiness suffers. The cumulative effect of the following words is to convince the reader that Mencken is incapable of being fair to Bryan or his admirers: <u>charlatan</u>, <u>mountebank</u>, <u>zany</u>, <u>clod</u>, <u>deluded</u>, <u>pathological hatred</u>, <u>half-wits</u>, <u>lusted</u>, <u>anthropoid rabble</u>, <u>malignancy</u>, <u>bawling</u>. All this is very obviously name calling.

EMOTIONAL APPEAL

The text acknowledges that emotional appeal is regarded by some "as an unworthy kind of persuasion." But your students know that people do react emotionally to issues and that emotions do influence decisions. They must decide what sorts of appeal to emotions they, as ethical writers, can allow themselves to use. When you raise the question, anticipate disagreement among class members.

<u>Discussion Problem</u> (pages 215-216)

Our students were not sharply divided in their judgments of the persuasiveness of "I Want a Wife." There was no conspicuous difference between the cumulative male reaction and the cumulative female reaction.

Most thought that the situation described in the essay is sufficiently typical to be credible, though one pointed out that the woman does not always keep the children after a divorce, and there was some feeling that the essay becomes less credible in the second half. This reaction grew from partial rejection of serious accusations made late in the essay, and also from annoyance at the repetition (thirty times) of I want a wife. The general reaction was that the writer belabors a worthy point.

The question arose of whether the writer was generalizing too much from unfortunate personal experience, though of course no one could answer this question. One young woman who has had most of the experiences attributed to the "wife" in the essay found the situation entirely credible and felt a kinship with the writer.

ARGUMENT

The third method of persuasion discussed in the chapter is argument. Some texts devote separate chapters to argument and to persuasion, or discuss persuasion under argument. In Writing with a Purpose argument is considered a major component of persuasion; the reasoning behind this belief is that a sound argument is perhaps the most persuasive device at the writer's command. Approximately one-third of the chapter on persuasion is devoted to argument, with subdivisions on (1) the structure of argument and (2) common types of arguments.

This edition of the text does not discuss the syllogism because (1) in freshman classes the intricacies of the syllogism are more confusing than helpful, and (2) as Toulmin's Uses of Argument shows, there are better ways of dealing with deductive arguments. (See page 172 in this Guide for a bibliographical entry.) The material on the structure of an argument concentrates on the relationship between premises and conclusions, an emphasis more practical for the freshman writer.

The material on common types of argument includes (a) types of premises (statement of fact, judgment, expert testimony) and (b) types of inferences (generalization, causal relation, causal generalization, and analogy). McCrimmon stresses that these types of argument must be used sensibly; each is valuable but must not be stretched beyond its ability to yield accurate conclusions.

You will particularly need to stress the limitation of arguing through analogy, for this method can easily deceive both the writer and the audience. For example, most of our students who saw the following analogy in the context of its argument approved of it.

> Professional football and professional boxing are contact sports.
>
> Increased safety equipment has not decreased the popularity of professional football.
>
> Increased safety equipment, such as head gear and more heavily padded gloves, would not decrease the popularity of professional boxing.

What readers of this analogy often overlook, when the analogy is not isolated as it is here, is that football and boxing differ significantly in the purposes of the participants. Football players win by running, passing, or kicking the ball over the goal line; safety equipment does not deter them from accomplishing their purpose. Professional boxers win by inflicting damage on their opponents, ideally by knocking them out; safety equipment, such as head gear and more heavily padded gloves, would deter them from accomplishing their purpose. Without knockouts, boxing might lose much of its popularity.

Exercise (pages 218-219)

A Yes in the answers below means that the two statements are related as premise and conclusion. A No means that they are not.

1a.	No	3a.	Yes
1b.	Yes	3b.	No
2a.	Yes	4a.	Yes
2b.	No	4b.	No

Discussion Problem (page 220)

Conclusion	We decided to replace the mule with a Volkswagen because
Premise 1	the VW better withstood extreme cold,
Premise 2	fuel for the VW was cheaper than feed for the mule,
Premise 3	the VW was less likely to get stuck in the mud,
Premise 4	the VW did not need a shelter,
Premise 5	the VW was easier to repair than the mule.

Exercise A (page 222)

1.
Conclusion	In practice we are not able to define heredity or environment with precision.
Main premise	We are not able to define heredity except in terms of characteristics that may have been influenced by environment.
Subpremise	Some inherited characteristics of fruit flies appear only when the environment encourages their appearance.
Subpremise	An acorn will never grow into anything but an oak tree, but whether it becomes an oak tree depends on environmental conditions.
Main premise	The environment of individuals in a society is so complex that we cannot define it precisely.

2.

Conclusion	We cannot study heredity or environment apart from each other.
Main premise	We cannot do this with newborn babies.
Subpremise	Newborn babies have had nine months of prenatal environment.
Main premise	We cannot do it with fraternal twins.
Subpremise	A boy twin has a different environment from that of a girl twin.
Main premise	We cannot do it with identical twins.
Subpremise	Identical twins come from the same egg and thus have the same inheritance, but we cannot be sure that they have had the same environment while growing up.

3.

Thesis: It is not possible to define or study heredity or environment apart from each other. (Conclusion from all premises)

I. In practice we cannot define either <u>heredity</u> or <u>environment</u>. (First main premise for thesis, but also a conclusion from A and B below)

   A. We are not able to define <u>heredity</u> except in terms of characteristics that may have been influenced by environment. (First premise for I above, but also a conclusion from 1 and 2 below)

      1. Some inherited characteristics of fruit flies appear only when the environment encourages their appearance. (First subpremise for A above)

      2. An acorn will never grow into anything but an oak tree, but whether it becomes an oak tree depends on environmental conditions. (Second subpremise for A above)

   B. The environment of individuals in a society is so complex that we cannot define it precisely. (Second premise for I above)

II. We cannot study heredity or environment apart from each other. (Second main premise for thesis, but also a conclusion from A, B, and C below)

   A. We cannot do it with newborn babies. (First premise for II, but also a conclusion from 1 below)

1. Newborn babies have had nine months of prenatal environment. (Subpremise for A above)

B. We cannot do it with fraternal twins. (Second premise for II, but also a conclusion from 1 below)

1. A boy twin has a different environment from that of a girl twin. (Subpremise for B above)

C. We cannot do it with identical twins. (Third premise for II, but also a conclusion from 1 below)

1. Identical twins come from the same egg and thus have the same inheritance, but we cannot be sure that they have had the same environment while growing up. (Subpremise for C above)

Some students may object to this outline because it has a single subpremise under II A, B, and C. They think there can be no single subdivisions. The objection would be sound if this were a classification outline, but in an outline of an argument there may be single subdivisions, since a conclusion may be drawn from only one premise. The outline above is an accurate structure of the total argument.

Exercise (page 225)

1. Premise: The sound of *a* in *ale* may also be spelled *ae* in *maelstrom*, *ai* in *bait*, *ay* in *day*, *e* and *ee* in *melee*, *ea* in *break*, *eigh* in *weigh*, *et* in *beret*.

   Conclusion: There is a tremendous lack of agreement between pronunciation and spelling in English.

   The premise is a statement of fact.

   The argument is persuasive, though *a tremendous* might better be replaced by *considerable* or *extensive*.

2. Premise: The letter *a* has different pronunciations in *sane*, *chaotic*, *care*, *add*, *account*, *arm*, *ask*, and *sofa*.

   Conclusion: The same letter may be used for different sounds.

   The premise is a statement of fact.

   The argument is entirely persuasive.

3. Premise: It is estimated that two-thirds of all the words in the Merriam-Webster unabridged dictionary have at least one silent letter.

Conclusion: English is full of silent letters.

The premise is a judgment. Since students have no way of evaluating that judgment without the testimony of an expert, who is not here identified, the accuracy of the premise cannot be established. The argument would be easier to accept if the conclusion were revised to read: "Silent letters are common in English."

4. Premise: George Bernard Shaw, who in addition to being a great playwright was a powerful advocate of simplified spelling, repeatedly stated his opinion in the London Times that by adopting simplified spelling Britain could have saved enough money to pay the costs of World War II.
Conclusion: The cost of typing, printing, and proofreading illogical spellings is high.

The premise is based on testimony.

Since Shaw was a biased witness on the subject of spelling reform and fond of making provocative statements, few readers would be willing to accept his word without corroborating evidence that illogical spelling cost as much as World War II. But they probably would accept the conclusion stated above.

Exercise A (page 227)

a. True in some cases.

b. True in most cases.

c. True in all cases. (To qualify they must be better-than-average swimmers; therefore, true by definition.)

d. True in some cases. (Some may insist that this statement is true in most cases. Unless an authoritative study can be cited, advocates of neither side will be able to prove their assertion.)

e. True in some cases.

f. True in most cases.

g. True in some cases.

h. True in some cases. (Some may insist that this statement is true in most cases.)

i. True in some cases. (An inquisitive student may be able to present data suggesting that the statement is true in most cases. If someone does, the class can enjoy evaluating the trustworthiness of the study.)

100 Teaching with a Purpose

Exercise B (pages 227-229)

Several characteristics of the article are worth noting.

The Testimony of Authority

The author cites a high-ranking officer in the U.S. Department of Health, Education, and Welfare to establish that something is wrong with "the distribution of health care" that Americans receive. A careful reader of this part of the article will note, though, that the official is not shown to have made any charge about incompetence of surgeons or maladministration of hospitals, the specific subjects that this article discusses.

Specificity--and the Lack of It

The reader can hardly avoid giving attention to the details about the malpractice of a particular surgeon and to the list of other offenses the author says he has discovered. On the other hand, the persuasiveness of the article suffers because neither the surgeon nor the hospitals in which offenses are said to have occurred are named.

The Nurse's Trustworthiness

Two significant paragraphs depend on the testimony of an unidentified nurse. The nurse's trustworthiness would be greater had the author made the point that she had a fine reputation among her colleagues. Her failure to report to medical authorities any of the doctor's alleged offenses damages her trustworthiness, though her coworkers' calling one situation to the attention of the hospital's chief of staff and his subsequent actions do lend credibility to her insistence that the doctor has been guilty of malpractice.

The Appeal to Emotion

The charges that people are enduring unnecessary operations and even dying as a result of the incompetence or dishonesty of doctors is certain to appeal to the emotions of almost any reader who accepts the writer's examples as true. Many Americans are willing to listen sympathetically to such charges, particularly if they or their families or friends have had direct experience with waiting a long time for brief attention from a doctor and then paying high fees for the service. On the other hand, some readers have objected to highly connotative language in the article. Examples are <u>specialized in diseases of the rich</u>, <u>adored by high-society patients</u>, and especially <u>butchered a number of patients</u>.

Typicality of the Case Cited

The author says that his investigation of "dozens of hospitals and clinics" has convinced him that the surgeon whom the nurse cited is not an isolated case. But there is a great difference between (1) not being an isolated case and (2) being a typical case. There is no convincing evidence in the text to show that the doctors referred to are typical.

Trustworthiness of the Author and the Publisher

Since most readers will not know the author's reputation, they will have to determine his trustworthiness largely on how well he has performed in the matters cited above. Some readers may question the credibility of the magazine that published the article. This question led to lively discussion and disagreement among the members of one group with whom we tested this material.

Exercise (pages 234-236)

Passage 1

Even though major surgery and impeachment are different in many ways, the care with which this analogy is constructed may make it persuasive, though as President Nixon's resignation shows, there is a "satisfactory alternative" in politics that could not exist in surgery.

Passage 2

This passage should provide the basis for a fine classroom discussion. The author is a prominent and controversial person writing about an important and controversial issue. Your students probably know Hayakawa's reputation as an outspoken Republican Senator from California. But they may not know that he is a well-known semanticist and that his "ringside seat" of the university affairs of which he speaks was the presidency of San Francisco State College, where he earned a reputation as a firm opponent of determined student rebels. Though Senator Hayakawa's background is too interesting to be ignored, you probably should not encourage discussion of it until the analogy itself has been examined. Then the question can arise of whether the past experience of the writer influences the persuasiveness of the piece.

Expect disagreement among students about the persuasiveness of the analogy. Their reactions may be influenced by their opinions about conditions on college campuses during the 1960s and 1970s and about government-funded social welfare programs. But encourage them to focus on questions concerning the analogy itself. Here are some that are appropriate; obviously, however, students cannot speak to all of them with confidence:

1. Are the effects of grade inflation and the effects of government-funded social welfare programs sufficiently similar to

form the basis for an analogy? Senator Hayakawa says, "You destroy not only education, you destroy society by giving A's to everyone."

2. a. Is it true that in the 1960s and 1970s there existed "a fashion of giving A's to every student," that "there were no failures," that "illiterate or lazy students could get an A average"? If so, did good students stop studying because of grade inflation?

   b. Are welfare recipients "assured of a comfortable living"? If so, does such assurance cause the average person to become a parasite on society? Are "parasites" present in both parts of the analogy?

3. a. Were "most of the dropouts" during this period "the most gifted and brilliant students"? If so, did they drop out because they "found that college had become meaningless"?

   b. Are "the brightest and most capable men and women" the "biggest losers" because of government welfare services? If so, are they losers in the way that "the most gifted and brilliant students" are said to have been losers?

4. Welfare officials, social workers, and politicians are cited as people with vested interests in welfare programs. Were there people (unnamed by Senator Hayakawa) other than students with vested interests in grade inflation in the 1960s and 1970s? If so, who were they, and are the two sets of vested interests analogous?

Suppose that some students answer yes to the first of these questions and no to one or more of the others--that is, they think the basis for the analogy is sound but are troubled by inconsistencies in parts of the analogy. In that case, they must decide whether the inconsistencies are crucial enough to damage seriously the effectiveness of the analogy.

REFUTING FALLACIES

New instructors, especially those fortunate enough to have had a college course in logic, are sometimes tempted to offer instruction in many more fallacies than composition students need to know by name. One adviser to new teachers reported that he listened to a first-term instructor--highly intelligent, enthusiastic, and well intentioned--introduce first-quarter freshman composition students to approximately twenty-five fallacies, many with Latin names, in about half an hour. The students could not have remembered most of them beyond the doorway.

This chapter presents only eleven fallacies, but they are basic ones. The emphasis is on becoming sensitive to illogical reasoning, not on attaching labels to fallacies. This sort of sensitivity should prove helpful in writing.

Discussion Problem (pages 243-245)

1. The statement about guilt is an unproved assertion. The explanation in no way fulfills the burden-of-proof requirement.

2. This reasoning begs the question. It assumes that the father will be alive four years from now and eligible for insurance. These assumptions may or may not turn out to be true. Should the father die before his children are through college and before he has purchased the insurance policy, the family may do much more skimping than the insurance premiums will necessitate if he buys the policy now and lives. The reasoning also ignores the possibility of the father's having to pay higher insurance rates when he may be less able to pay them (in retirement) if he delays purchasing the policy.

3. The large vocabularies may be a contributory cause or one of several causes for people's success. Almost certainly they are not the only cause. Perhaps, too, more intelligent people (1) have larger vocabularies and (2) are more successful than less intelligent people. Intelligence, rather than just large vocabularies, may be responsible for success. The argument may, then, mistake an effect for a cause.

4. The argument begs the question by assuming that the high divorce rate in teenage marriages is caused by immaturity. This assumption has to be proved. Other causes may be lack of financial resources and interference from parents who think the "children" are too young to be married.

5. The either-or fallacy is at work here. Other alternatives are possible. Perhaps the university can recruit athletes capable of meeting present academic standards, or the teams may play less rigorous schedules without the school's sinking "into athletic oblivion."

6. This argument relies on a faulty analogy. The skills of a good mechanic and the skills of a good writer are too different for excellence in one set of skills to be used to predict excellence in the other.

7. The writer has formed a hasty generalization, having drawn a conclusion about all the students in the school on the basis of two experiences involving a very few students.

8. The writer has mistaken one of several causes for a sole cause. There are other reasons humankind has survived: reasoning power, ability to build shelter, and ability to make and use tools, for example.

9. B is guilty of the fallacy of extension. A made no criticism of the South, Faulkner, O'Connor, McCullers, or any other Southern writer except Wolfe. Furthermore, A did not deny Wolfe's spontaneity or lyricism, and even acknowledged that Wolfe was sometimes "very good." A criticized only Wolfe's verbosity.

10. This is an example of <u>argumentum ad hominem</u> applied to women. The speaker makes no effort to evaluate what the women said. Instead, he responds with a personal and emotional objection to their looks and in the process makes an unsupported judgment that they hate men. This kind of emotional reaction can hardly be justified as argument.

11. The either-or-fallacy once more. Between the extreme positions that Europe should pay all of the costs of the European part of the program or else the United States should pull out, there is plenty of room for negotiations to determine a fair share of the costs of a program that is designed to protect both Europe and the United States.

12. This is an oversimplified cause that attributes a complex result to a simple cause. Considering the social, economic, and political reasons for the student demonstrations of the 1960s, it is difficult to believe that the alleged "permissive theories" of Dr. Spock explain all the reasons. If the speaker thinks they do, he must do much more than he has done to establish an acceptable causal relation.

13. This is a hasty generalization. On the evidence of one letter by one student, the employer generalizes that the state university does not deserve the tax support it is getting. We would need to have much more evidence than he offers to accept that conclusion.

14. This analogy will not bear examination. There are two reasons why one cannot prove that football is not dangerous by citing death statistics: (1) teenagers and young adults do not die as frequently as infants and old people; (2) since football players must pass physical examinations before they can play, one would expect them to be healthier than nonplayers. Moreover, football players can be seriously and permanently injured without dying from their injuries.

15. This argument assumes that because two things exist together--sex education and venereal disease--the first is the cause of the second. No evidence is offered to support the assumed causal connection.

16. Several questions arise. What are the "moral standards of the community"? If they have been established, has there been a study by competent people establishing that the banned novels offend those standards? If so, are the books necessarily pornographic? Are we certain that pornography "corrupts the minds and morals of the young"? Are we certain that the causes of mental and moral corruption can be located and stamped out as the causes of typhoid can be? This paragraph is a mixture of question begging and unexamined analogy.

17. The writer has made a hasty generalization. The conclusion about all English cooking is based on one meal in one restaurant and the meals served on one voyage on one ship.

18. The reasoning is based on unsupported assumptions: that educated people make wiser decisions than do uneducated people, that an educational system generously supported is better than one not generously supported, that better educational systems produce wiser citizens than do less good systems, and that wise citizens contribute to the welfare of the state. Therefore, in a democracy, where the citizens must choose between alternatives, education is the "fundamental problem." Perhaps all these assumptions can be demonstrated to be true. But in the material we are given, there are no such demonstrations. The writer ignores the burden of proof and begs the question. Too, the reasoning is very close to being circular.

Review Exercise A (pages 245-247)

The purpose of the assignment is not only to select the better paper but also to give students practice in looking closely at arguments and evaluating them. Our experience with contests like this one is that they generate considerable difference of opinion. Usually, every paper is considered the best by some students and the worst by others, and if more than two papers are involved, sometimes no paper wins majority support. Since these two essays were chosen to make a decision difficult, you can expect disagreement. The observations below may give helpful background for class discussion.

Paper 1: "A New Look at an Old Myth"

This paper is chiefly an effect-to-cause argument. It begins with two paragraphs that set up contrasting effects (oversupply of workers in jobs requiring a college degree and undersupply in some other occupations). Paragraph 3 relates these effects to what is alleged to be their cause, the myth that a college degree is a passport to prosperity. Paragraph 4 cites other evils alleged to come from the same cause--dropouts, failures, expense of time and money, and blasted hopes. Then in paragraphs 5 and 6 the paper suggests alternatives to going directly from high school to college. The final paragraph makes an emotional appeal to stop the harm the myth causes by emphasizing acceptable alternatives. The structure of the essay is almost standard for an argument to remove an evil:

1. Show the undesirable effects.

2. Identify the cause of these effects.

3. Remove the cause and therefore the effects by substituting an acceptable alternative.

Students who choose this paper as a winner may be influenced by the following: the originality of the thesis for a college freshman; the force with which the thesis is maintained; the emotional material about dropouts, failures, and students brainwashed into going to college; the positive suggestions about alternatives;

and the implication that the writer is acting out of a sincere concern for the welfare of young people and is therefore trustworthy.

Students who reject this paper may do so because they are committed to a belief in the economic value of a college education and think that the author has overstated his case; or they may feel that the whole argument rests largely on the unsupported opinions of the writer and needs the support of expert testimony and more specific and documented evidence about the <u>relative</u> opportunities for employment among those who have a college degree and those who have not.

Paper 2: "DDT Should Be Banned from All Use"

This paper created a great deal of controversy among our students, largely because an exceptionally well-informed environmentalist attacked the writer's trustworthiness on the basis that what she says is partly erroneous. Other students who thought the writer had competently discussed an important subject defended the essay. The paper's emotional appeal, certainly one of its assets, may have influenced these people. The emotional appeal and persuasiveness of the paper are enhanced by the fine introduction. One does not often find in student writing an introductory statement that sets the tone for a paper as well as this one does. Another good quality is that the student speaks with conviction about a most significant problem.

Here are some of the questions that our students raised, even though most thought the paper was quite good:

1. Should <u>all</u> use of DDT be banned? The writer acknowledges that "DDT has saved perhaps millions of lives by reducing the spread of malaria." Is there no desirable alternative between unrestricted use and no use?

2. Twice the writer mentions "<u>the</u> food chain," and she says that "man occupies the top level of the food chain." Is there only one food chain? (People do not normally eat eagles and hawks.)

3. Couldn't the writer have made her paper more persuasive by citing expert testimony? Such testimony is available.

These criticisms do not negate the considerable appeal of the paper. You may find your students widely divided in their opinions of its persuasiveness.

SOME FINAL STATEMENTS ABOUT PROBLEMS IN PERSUASION PAPERS

1. Most students have had little experience in planning the strategy of a paper. Finding common ground with a reader, demonstrating an understanding of opposing arguments, and making clear what one is <u>not</u> speaking about if the subject of the paper is likely to be misunderstood--these are tactics that most of your students do not know about consciously. ("Three Points

of View," pages 20-22, is a paper that can be most helpful as you discuss strategy.)

2. A few students may think a persuasion unit is intended to teach them how to twist information so that it fools, and thereby persuades, the audience. You will want to take care to disillusion such students of this impression. One way to do this is to require your students to write for audiences sufficiently perceptive to detect deception.

3. Students sometimes choose audiences whom they are not competent to address. One young woman wanted to address an international convention of Old Testament scholars on the validity of miracles. She could not qualify for this role, but she did know a good deal about the Old Testament and so could comfortably address her undergraduate class in religion on her subject. If a student chooses a suitable audience other than the class, fine. But rather than allowing her to speak to an audience she is not qualified to address, suggest that she address the class.

4. Students' choosing unusually informal occasions for their persuasion papers can present special problems. Suppose a young woman is talking to six of her dorm mates as they sip Cokes in the lounge. She wants to persuade them of the need for some changes in dorm rules. It is not realistic to expect that her friends will remain quiet while she lectures. They will interrupt to agree, disagree, and propose alternatives. Is the student prepared to write this sort of dialogue? And are you willing to accept a persuasion paper in the form of dialogue?

5. A student with strong, deep-rooted emotions about a subject should consider carefully whether to attempt a persuasive paper on that subject. Angry or inaccurate statements that grow out of strong emotion can seriously damage a writer's credibility.

6. You will need to emphasize that in a persuasion paper the thesis is a debatable proposition. A formal statement of the thesis cannot begin with "I think . . . " or "This paper will discuss . . . "; such statements are not debatable.

PART 3

SPECIAL ASSIGNMENTS

CHAPTER 10   THE ESSAY EXAMINATION

Many freshmen have had little or no experience in writing essay examinations, and few have had instruction in how to write them. A college instructor should recognize this situation and try to understand the panic the student experiences when asked in an examination session to analyze and interpret, to compare and contrast, or to discover symbolic patterns. With limited information about the subject and no methodology to fall back on, the student is likely to strike out in all directions, writing down whatever comes to mind--all the time frantically aware that all too soon time will be up.

This chapter can help students avoid this sort of terror. It gives four pieces of practical advice intended to improve their ability to write essay examinations:

1. Read the question carefully.

2. Think out your answer before writing.

3. Write a complete answer.

4. Do not pad your answer.

WRITING ON THE ASSIGNMENT

The following case illustrates the difficulty of some students in deciding exactly what the question calls for and then writing on the assignment. A young man was supposed to explain the function of superstition in Adventures of Huckleberry Finn. His response to the problem began with "In Huckleberry Finn there is an aura of superstition and magic that helps to make the book enjoyable to read." Then he named several superstitions without showing how they function in the novel. By line count, exactly 75 percent of the paper summarized the action of the book without reference to superstition; but the closing sentence read, "All in all, the flavor of superstition and magic add much to the enjoyment of reading the book." Though his instructor made a specific recommendation for the student to recover (by writing a satisfactory discussion) from the damage the essay had done to his standing in the course, this performance had to be rated less than satisfactory. His paper was not written primarily about the subject he was supposed to discuss.

The instructor's experience with this young man's essay is unusual only in degree, not in kind. Students often write on a subject other than the one an examination question requires—sometimes for lack of information, sometimes for lack of experience. Some may even have been rewarded for this practice in the past. Their high school teachers were probably burdened with unreasonable teaching loads and so quite understandably may have felt that trying to read papers closely was futile. The reasonably well-informed student who wrote passably well on something resembling what the question called for may have received an A or a B, along with "Good work."

You probably should be slow to assure your students that those days are behind them. They may go through course after course in college without being required to write essay examinations or without having their work read carefully. But if a student is fortunate, he or she may study with several professors who take seriously the preparing and marking of essay examinations, and it is for these professors' courses that you are trying to prepare your students in this unit. A summary will not do when an analysis is asked for, nor will an analysis of a subject other than the one the question is about. In these courses, misreading the problem (either deliberately or unconsciously) is a sure beginning toward an unsatisfactory mark.

PLANNING THE EXAMINATION ANSWER

It is common for students writing essay examinations to race off to a quick start as soon as the questions are read, without doing any planning. Students who write this way often think of valuable points after they have written past the places where these points belong. They may begin the last paragraph with something like "One might also add . . . ." It is often painfully obvious that "one" should have "added" this information much earlier in the essay.

The solution to this sort of problem is simple. The students can simply list the ideas pertinent to the question and decide which of these are main ideas and which are subordinate. These relationships can be indicated by arrows running from the subordinate ideas to the main ones. The students may discover that some ideas do not belong, and scratch them out. Then they have only to decide on the most reasonable order for the main ideas and to number them accordingly before they are ready to start writing. This procedure has three advantages over the "quick start" method: (1) the writer is not distracted by composing while generating ideas; (2) once an idea is down in note form it cannot be forgotten; and (3) with the planning done, the writer can concentrate on clear expression during the actual writing.

Time spent in planning the essay examination answer is not time lost. The rough outlines enable students to use their writing time economically, and so they are likely to have a few minutes left to proofread their work. A reasonable division of time in a fifty-minute examination period is about ten minutes for planning, approximately thirty-five minutes for writing, and about five minutes for proofreading.

WRITING A COMPLETE ANSWER, BUT NOT PADDING THE ESSAY

In most college writing the student is expected to know what his or her thesis is and to develop it fully and logically. These requirements are particularly applicable to writing examinations; the reader knows what generalizations the writer should reach, what specifics are available to support them, and what logical relationships exist among the specifics and the generalizations. You can emphasize that no basic principle of good writing has changed here; rather, a changed relationship between the reader and the writer's material has made writing a complete answer particularly important in this writing situation.

Some students write incomplete answers to examination questions because they have never learned the value of thinking for a few minutes to discover what they know. Others write incomplete answers near the end of a multi-problem essay examination because they have spent too much time on the early problems. You will need to emphasize the importance of budgeting time throughout an examination period. Of course, some students fail to write full answers because they simply do not have the information necessary to discuss the problems. Uninformed students may write a few sentences and quit, or they may write fully, but on a subject somewhat different from the one the question requires them to discuss. Or students may write on the assigned subject but pad the answer by saying the same thing in different ways.

But the padded answer does not always grow from a lack of information. It may result from a lack of planning. Or the student may have learned through the years that a long answer tends to get a high grade. One instructor tells about a potentially excellent student who wrote spectacularly unplanned and padded answers. She wrote the way she thought and talked--very, very fast. Given thirty minutes on an essay question, she would hand in about eight full pages. There was no attempt to cover up what she did not know, for she was exceptionally well informed. All the information necessary for an A answer would be in her essay, and more--and stated more than once. Like the lovely woman in Theodore Roethke's poem, this young woman's essay "moved in circles, and those circles moved." Apparently no one had ever before done anything except praise her writing. Finally, in frustration over B grades on examinations, she told her instructor as courteously as she could something like this: "I have always just written and written and written, and you're the first person who ever told me I didn't know what I was doing!" She was perfectly capable of disciplined writing; her problem was that no one had ever required it of her.

SOME SUGGESTIONS FOR DEVELOPING AND USING ESSAY EXAMINATION QUESTIONS

(Note: The following suggestions are intended for teachers who are beginning their careers. Experienced teachers are likely to have already developed practices similar to the ones recommended here.)

1. Consider whether you need to check for general knowledge of a broad subject or for detailed mastery of a relatively narrow subject. Be sure that what you expect the students to do can be accomplished within the amount of time available.

2. If you have an hour for the examination, should you ask the students to write one relatively long essay or two or three shorter ones? If they are to write several short discussions, remember that they need time to think through each problem. Much bad writing on essay examinations results from the students' having to write on too many problems within a strict time limit.

3. Give careful thought to the level of difficulty of your questions. Even good students usually do not know as much as a young teacher expects them to know.

4. Decide what sort of strategy you want your students to employ. Should they compare and contrast, explain a cause-and-effect relationship, summarize? Be certain that the subject matter lends itself to the sort of discussion you require.

5. Take care to word the problems carefully. To get well into marking a set of papers and realize that the unsatisfactory essays are the result of a poorly worded question is a frustrating experience for a teacher.

6. Whenever practical, give your students choices among problems that they may write on. What seems a reasonable question to the instructor does not always strike even able and conscientious students as reasonable. Your giving students options will help prevent this sort of difficulty.

7. Be sure you have a clear idea of the information (and other characteristics) you expect in a good response to a question. If you have not used the question before, outline a good answer to it before you assign the problem. You may discover difficulties that suggest altering or dropping the question.

8. If you have not used particular questions before, you may need responses from a number of students in order to feel confident in your evaluation of the papers. You can avoid having only two or three papers on each of several questions by restricting the number of problems from which your students may choose.

9. Consider whether you want your students to make any specific preparation for the examination. Will you give them study questions that are related, but not identical, to the ones they will write on? Should they bring notes to the examination?

A brief outline for a particular discussion? Or should you have them come to the examination session without any specific information about problems? Do not rule out quickly the possibility of allowing students to make some specific preparation under guidelines you prescribe, particularly if you are going to expect a significant piece of work from them during the examination hour. If you do allow students to bring notes or outlines to the examination, explain that it is absolutely necessary for them not to bring more than your guidelines allow. Otherwise, a seriously inequitable situation can develop.

10. Will you allow students to stay a few minutes after class to continue writing? If so, be sure that every student has an equal opportunity to perform well. A student who has no class next hour must not be given an advantage over one who does.

11. When you evaluate essay examinations you are particularly aware of the content-versus-correctness issue. Think carefully about what your purposes are for giving the examination and what is reasonable to expect of the students. You probably should avoid both extremes in deciding how much correctness in composition skills should count in this particular kind of writing. Be sure your students know before they write what criteria you will use when you evaluate their papers.

12. After you have graded a set of essay examinations, evaluate the questions very critically in the light of the writing they yielded. Were any too easy to measure what you wanted to test? Did competent students find any too demanding? Did a question invite vague responses? Drop or carefully revise those that did not work well so they will not cause difficulty in another term.

Discussion Problem (pages 261, 263-267)

Question 1

The major difference between these two answers is that the first ignores the examiner's directions, and the second follows them. The directions require the writer to "discuss the contribution of William Morris to book design," using his <u>Chaucer</u> as an example. The first answer does not focus on that purpose. Instead, the first half of the paragraph describes some features of Morris's <u>Chaucer</u>, without relating these features to their contribution to book designing. The second half slides into a digression on Morris's contribution to home furnishings, which is not related to the examiner's directions.

In contrast, the second answer deals exclusively with the relation of Morris's <u>Chaucer</u> to the improvement of book designing in printing. The first two sentences explicitly state Morris's intention to raise the standards of printing. The next three sentences identify features of his <u>Chaucer</u> that made it a work of art or high craft and therefore showed what printers could do to improve the quality of their work. The concluding sentence states the effect of the book on other printers and so rounds out a purposeful answer to the examiner's directions.

Question 2

The first answer is more effective than the second as an explanation of the difference between neurosis and psychosis, because it provides a more detailed contrast of both terms. The first paragraph establishes the basic difference as a thesis, the second explains neurosis in detail, the third gives equal attention to psychosis, and the fourth concludes the contrast. The whole answer is a good example of the A+B contrast discussed on pages 67-68.

The writer of the second essay has the basic understanding needed for writing a satisfactory response to the question. The second sentence of the first paragraph states that "[the psychotic] is less likely [than the neurotic] to be aware of what he is doing." And the second sentence of the second paragraph reads in part, "if a neurotic condition becomes so serious that the person is out of touch with the real world and locked into his private world, he is psychotic." So the problem is not that the writer does not have the basic information necessary for speaking to the assignment.

Part of the problem is that the writer has spoken to an imaginary assignment that might have read, "Cite several defense mechanisms that neurotic persons may use in their struggles with their frustrations." Most of the essay discusses this subject. The writer says little about psychosis and gives only passing attention to the strategy that the assignment requires, that of contrasting two concepts.

Question 3

The second of the two essays on the two paintings is not so weak as the second of the two discussions of neurosis and psychosis. It seems particularly inadequate only when compared with its excellent companion. The poorer essay shows "the difference between early and late Renaissance painting" only implicitly. There is nothing in it to compare with the transition through contrast in the first essay that leads the reader from the first paragraph into the second. Nor is there sufficient data in the weaker essay to justify this summarizing comparison used in the stronger discussion: "Where Filippo's work is mere copying, Raphael's is imaginative and spiritual." Finally, the second essay does not show so clearly as the first that the characteristics of the two paintings are typical of painting in the two periods, though certainly it is not a total failure in this respect. We are speaking here about the differences between an excellent and a mediocre paper, not between an excellent and a poor paper.

CHAPTER 11   THE CRITICAL ESSAY: WRITING ABOUT LITERATURE

Because the chapter on writing the critical essay about literature is long and contains a variety of material, an overview can be useful as you plan your work with the chapter. There are three basic divisions in the chapter: "Prewriting the Critical Essay," "Questions of Emphasis," and "Writing the Paper."

PREWRITING THE CRITICAL ESSAY (pages 270-291)

This section discusses ten basic elements of imaginative writing that the student needs to know before writing about literature. These are situation, character, plot, dramatic conflict, theme, structure, symbol, irony, point of view, and voice. A number of the examples that illustrate these elements are drawn from Ralph Ellison's "King of the Bingo Game," which is printed in its entirety. After the author has analyzed this story closely in his discussion of the nine elements, he leads the student through an analysis of William Saroyan's story "Snake" as a demonstration of prewriting an interpretive paper.

QUESTIONS OF EMPHASIS (pages 291-299)

This section discusses three basic operations in the critical process: technical analysis, interpretation, and evaluation. The material on technical analysis stresses that a reader should interpret only after analyzing the work carefully. A paper in the technical analysis subsection ("The Detached Interpreter," pages 294-295) is an excellent example of how an essay can be developed from a carefully developed study guide (page 294) that requires the writer to analyze a poem carefully in the prewriting stage of an essay about the poem. The chapter does not advocate adherence to any particular theory of literary criticism, but it does insist that a valid interpretation must be consistent with what happens in the literary work. The subsection on evaluation contains a short article that makes a judgment about Salinger's The Catcher in the Rye. McCrimmon discusses this article, showing how the writer invites the reader's confidence in her evaluation.

117

118   Teaching with a Purpose

WRITING THE PAPER (pages 300-305)

Because the writing of a critical essay is not substantially different from the writing process that has been presented in detail in Part I, the advice here focuses on the following six points:

1. Make clear to your readers what your real subject is.

2. Select and evaluate your material.

3. Summarize the work when necessary.

4. Use quotations when they help, but do not overuse them.

5. Use source references if necessary.

6. Always proofread your finished essay carefully.

SNAKE (pages 285-290)

After Saroyan's "Snake," McCrimmon leads the student through an interpretation and analysis of the story that should help the student to participate in the critical process. The reading below is intended to suggest key ideas and phrases that you almost certainly can use as you lead a class discussion of "Snake." In parentheses there are some statements and questions that may be helpful as you work with some of the more puzzling problems in the story.

<u>The Young Man and the Snake</u>

The snake is the symbol of evil, the young man says.

He considers claiming to be a student of contemporary morality if anyone discovers him in the park toying with the snake. (And so the reader is alerted to one possible subject for the story.) The young man resolves that he will not tell other people that he intends to kill the snake.

He thinks that "to touch a snake [is] to touch something secret in the mind of man, something one ought never to bring out into the light." (His experience will teach him differently; still later he will even be able to relate the experience to the young woman.)

The young man feels as if he is alone with the snake in the Garden of Eden.

He feels that he has "an obligation to man" to destroy the snake. (If he does this, evil will never be able to leave the Garden and plague mankind.)

In addition to singing a lullaby and whistling a song containing the words <u>my only love</u>, he sings to the snake, as he taunts it with a stick, "Woman is fickle." (In Verdi's <u>Rigoletto</u> the Duke, who sings about the fickleness of woman, is tragically mistaken. The Duke is responsible for the death of a faithful young woman.)

He intends to kill the snake, "To destroy that evil grace, to mangle that sinful loveliness." But he changes his mind and says, "I have only love for you."

He picks up the snake and discovers its "true feel"--cold and clean--and drops it. He thought it would be slimy.

He tells the snake that it has "been in the presence of man" and is "yet alive." He tells the snake to return to its kind and to tell them what it saw and felt. He says that the snake's having met man will bring it distinction. (For once man does not kill.)

The Young Man and the Young Woman

The young man tells the young woman, who is playing the piano, about his seeing the snake. She says, "How ugly!" He says, "No. It was beautiful." He says it felt clean.

He says he "wanted to kill the snake" but couldn't because it was "too lovely." She is glad that he found the snake to be lovely and clean and that he could not kill it.

She insists several times on being told everything about his encounter with the snake.

He says he "was going to kill the snake, and not come here again." (Could he thereby destroy the symbol and then avoid the reality of evil? But he did not kill the snake, and he has come to the young woman again.)

She insists on knowing what association he made between her and the snake. He answers, "I thought you were lovely but evil." (In Genesis it is the woman who is beguiled by the snake into eating of the Tree of Knowledge and who then persuades the man to do the same.)

He asks her what his "picking up the snake" means. She evades his question. He has confidence that she knows Freudian psychology. (Is he Innocence and she Knowledge, even though it is he who has encountered the snake? If so, twice he has encountered a symbol associated with knowledge without experiencing harm. The snake did strike out at him, but ineffectually and only in defense.)

He thinks "it was very fine to let the snake go free." (Does he also think it is fine that he has come to see the young woman again?)

She asks whether he has ever told her that he loves her. He evades her question. She says he hasn't, but she laughs because she feels "very happy about him." She says he has "always talked of other things," of "irrelevant things," and "at the most amazing times." (When he could have been professing his love for her?) He seems to continue his practice now, saying that the snake "was a little brown snake." She says (not in response to what he has just said), "And that explains it. You have never intruded." (Do his unwillingness to intrude and his tactic of talking about irrelevant matters explain why he has never told her he loves her? Does his unwillingness to kill (intrude upon) the lovely snake explain his unwillingness to declare his love for her, which would amount to intruding on her and in a sense killing, by possessing, a part of her? Does his fear that she is evil explain his unwillingness to risk intruding on her loveliness?) He asks what she is talking about. She doesn't answer but says, "I'm so glad you didn't kill the snake." (Though he still has not declared his love for her, by now she must realize that his sparing the snake and his coming to see her again are indicative of his desire to continue his relationship with her.)

She returns to her piano. He tells her that he "whistled a few songs to the snake." He says he would like to hear the part of a song "that goes, you are my only love, my only love." (This is the song he whistled to the snake. There is no mention of "Woman is fickle" now.)

She begins to play, presumably the song he has requested, and feels his eyes "studying her as he had studied the snake." (Is he discovering that she, too, is lovely and clean--though warm, not cold like the snake? That she is not slimy and evil?)

(This reading of the story suggests an inversion of the conventional symbolic meaning of the snake.)

The following excerpts[1] from Genesis include the parts of the Garden of Eden story most directly relevant to "Snake."

The Snake in the Garden

Now the snake was more subtile than any beast of the field which the Lord God had made. And he said unto the woman, Yea, hath God said, Ye shall not eat of every tree of the garden? And the woman said unto the serpent, We may eat of the fruit of the trees of the garden: But of the fruit of the tree which is in the midst of the garden, God hath said, Ye shall not eat of it, neither shall ye touch it, lest ye die. And the serpent said unto the woman, Ye shall not surely die: For God doth know that in the day ye eat thereof, then your eyes shall be opened, and ye shall be as gods, knowing good and evil.

Genesis 3:1-5

1. From The Dartmouth Bible, edited by Roy B. Chamberlin and Herman Feldman (Boston: Houghton Mifflin, 1950).

The Critical Essay: Writing About Literature

> And the Lord God said unto the woman,
> What is this that thou hast done? And the woman
> said, The serpent beguiled me, and I did eat.
> And the Lord God said unto the serpent,
>
> Because thou hast done this, thou art cursed above
>   all cattle, and above every beast of the field;
> upon thy belly shalt thou go,
>   and dust shalt thou eat all the days of thy life:
> And I will put enmity between thee and the woman,
>   and between thy seed and her seed;
> it shall bruise thy head,
>   and thou shalt bruise his heel.
>
> Genesis 3:13-15

Exercise A (page 291)

1. The question of what would have happened later had the young man killed the snake should lead students to compare events in the two parts of the story and to realize the relationship between the story's structure and its meaning.

    If the young man had killed the snake, he might not have visited the young woman again ("I was going to kill the snake, and not come here again"). If he had gone to her, certainly the visit would not have been the pleasant occasion that it was, for he would have associated the snake and the young woman with evil. He could not have requested that she play the tune to <u>you are my only love, my only love</u>.

    Because the story (as well as the Genesis account) clearly invites the reader to see a relationship between the snake and the woman, some students may decide that if the man had killed the snake, he would have had to kill her. Remind these students that the story need not be read as an allegory in which the snake and the woman must be treated identically. Ask them to consider the effect (a particular kind of killing) of his not returning to her once he had killed the snake.

2. If Saroyan had assigned more specific identities to the man and the woman, the reader might be slower to see them as modern Adam and Eve or as representatives of humankind. (The effect of keeping them nameless is similar to that achieved by Ellison in "King of the Bingo Game," where he assigns no name to his main character.)

3. The woman may be saying merely that the man is an idiot for taking the snake in his hand. Or she may be suggesting that it was idiocy for him ever to have associated her with the snake and evil. Whatever her meaning, she speaks to him in good humor; she is relieved that he did not kill the snake, and she laughs softly and says, "Why, it's splendid" when he tells her that he picked up the snake.

4. The reading of the story presented above provides more information to support the partial interpretation presented in the text. But do not give the students the additional information too quickly; let them do most of the analysis and interpretation.

5. Do not discourage students from disagreeing with the interpretation presented in the text and guide as long as they are relying on patterns of evidence consistent with what happens in the story. If you feel that some are determined to force the story to take on meanings they arrived at before doing a thorough job of analysis, you may want to return briefly to this exercise after you have worked with the "Hunting Song" materials (pages 293-295 and 296-297 in the text and herein below); these materials emphasize that an interpretation should grow out of careful analysis of the literary work and (in "Symbolism in 'Hunting Song'") show the result of the writer's arriving at an interpretation too soon.

THE "HUNTING SONG" MATERIALS (pages 293-295)

The study questions that accompany "Hunting Song" and the essay ("The Detached Interpreter") on the poem can be useful as you encourage your students to analyze before they interpret. Notice that the essay has been considerably influenced by the study questions. The following correlation table makes the point.

Study Questions	Essay Paragraphs
1	2
2	3
3	4, 5
4	5, 6
5	1 and throughout paper

Carefully developed study questions can be most helpful in teaching students how to let their interpretation and evaluation grow from analysis. The study questions for "Hunting Song" are designed to teach students how to read the poem discriminatingly and to lead them to a justifiable interpretation.

As you work with "The Detached Interpreter" you can show the relationship between the opening and closing of the essay--two sections of a paper that cause students much trouble. At the same time you can demonstrate that the writer was keenly aware of the dependence of interpretation on analysis. The first paragraph explains the bases on which the study of the poem is to be made, and the last clause of this paragraph indicates that the poem makes a statement "about the living and the dead" (a matter that the last three paragraphs will discuss). Then the writer presents his analysis for several paragraphs. This analysis enables him to suggest in the last two paragraphs that the dead, unlike the living, need not become emotionally involved with events that are merely temporary. They are emotionally detached and so can view the excited hurrying of the living "with sublime detachment."

Some of your students may know Thorton Wilder's play <u>Our Town</u> (often included in high school anthologies and reading lists), which makes a point similar to the one the author of "The Detached Interpreter" sees in "Hunting Song." In Act III the dead in the play, like the log in "Hunting Song," are emotionally detached from events that the living think are urgent. The Stage Manager introduces a scene that occurs in the Grover's Corner cemetery, where the community's dead are sitting in chairs. He says to the audience,

> You know as well as I do that the dead don't stay interested in us living people very long. Gradually, gradually, they let hold of the earth . . . .

There is a striking similarity between the Stage Manager's belief that the dead "get weaned away from the earth" and the thought expressed in "The Detached Interpreter" that the log is "so long dead that he is free from involvement in temporal matters and so can watch the chase with sublime detachment."

You can generate interest in interpretation by bringing this similarity into your class discussion. Or you may want to give students who already know the play, and so would need to reread only the third act, the opportunity to write a comparative paper on this particular similarity between the two works. The following are possible subjects:

The detachment of the dead in two works

Involvement in temporal affairs

Two statements about the living and the dead

<u>Discussion Problem</u> (pages 296-297)

The student who wrote "Symbolism in 'Hunting Song'" was a member of a class asked to write about the poem without the instructor's offering any guidelines for analysis and interpretation. Almost all the students saw that they must pay close attention to the log. But their many interpretations of what the log means varied from the Cross of the Crucifixion to a house of prostitution. (The student who offered the latter interpretation pointed out that a bitch found the fox's scent and was chasing him into her house. This student ignored, among other conditions of the poem, the fact that the fox and the hound were running <u>away</u> from the log.)

The following analysis of the interpretation in "Symbolism in 'Hunting Song'" points out that the interpretation in this paper grows from faulty analysis and so is an unsatisfactory reading. Some of your students will object to the critique, for they do not believe that there is such a thing as a bad reading of a poem. Some think that a poem says whatever any reader decides it means to him or her. (It is probably better to disillusion these students gradually and gently with close readings of several poems rather than abruptly through a direct statement, for some become quite emotional about the matter.)

The first two paragraphs of "Symbolism in 'Hunting Song'" indicate that the writer knows that the poem has "a deeper meaning than a mere fox hunt." Though the reader may be somewhat puzzled by the suggestion of a "moving incident of religious belief" at the end of the first paragraph, he or she will sense that the student is raising an appropriate question by asking "But what does it all mean?" at the end of the second paragraph.

The reader may suspect trouble when the writer says in paragraph three that the word <u>song</u> in the poem's title suggests the "Song of Solomon." Why this association rather than "Song of Hiawatha," "Song of Roland," "Song of the Islands," or any number of other songs? If indeed the poem does suggest "a religious feeling" and so a song from the Bible, why Solomon's song rather than David's, Moses', Miriam's, or another? The mildly erotic "Song of Solomon" is not religious except in a metaphorical sense. Certainly one can read the eight chapters of this Old Testament book without finding any clue that would associate it with the Crucifixion of Christ. The student's decision in paragraph three is basic to this interpretation of the poem, and that decision is suspect.

In paragraph four the writer announces that the fox, who is "like death at the end of a string," is "the redheaded Judas." Admittedly, the animal could be a red fox, and Judas did indeed hang until dead from "the end of a string." But surely the writer errs in saying that Judas "lolled about"; he would not have been that relaxed at a time when he was betraying his Master and would soon hang himself. And even if he did loll, the fox doesn't. Judas's lolling would not have been similar to the fox's running; the student probably has confused <u>to loll</u> with <u>to lollop</u>. Too, it is difficult to see that the fox's running "in one side and out of the other" is comparable to Judas's "kiss of betrayal." Finally, the writer says Judas moved "right along with the crowd," but the fox is running <u>from</u> the crowd of hounds.

In the fifth paragraph the student explains that some in the crowd "stood with 'their heads . . . low and their eyes . . . red'" because they "were ashamed of their actions." In the poem the dogs hold their heads low because they are following a scent, not because they are ashamed. And the redness in their eyes is natural for hounds. Furthermore, there is no suggestion in the Biblical story that the women weeping for Jesus have taken any part in demanding his crucifixion, and so it is inappropriate to suggest that they are ashamed of their actions. Still another inconsistency exists in this paragraph. The student seems to say that the crowd follows Jesus, as indeed they do in the Biblical account. But apparently the writer has forgotten momentarily that the crowd (the hounds) in the poem are following the "symbol" for Judas (the fox).

In paragraph six the writer sees the hunter as royalty, as emperor, as Pilate. (Pilate was, of course, a governor, not an emperor.) The student says the hunter is wearing "the red coat of royalty"; purple, not red, is the color of royalty. (In the

Biblical story no reference is made to the color of Pilate's clothing; the Roman soldiers dress Christ in a purple cloak and a crown of thorns to mock what they interpret as his claim to being a king.) In the last half of the paragraph the student refers to Pilate's washing his hands of responsibility for Christ's death. There is no parallel reference in the poem to the hunter's washing his hands, but one suspects that the writer sees the symbolic Pilate cleansing himself in horse sweat, an unlikely cleansing agent. In the New Testament story Pilate washes his hands <u>in front of</u> the multitude; in the poem the hunter is <u>chasing after</u> the hounds.

In the last paragraph the writer suggests that the final stanza of the poem requires close reading, and this is right. But then the writer announces abruptly that the log is a symbol for the Cross and says that Christ is on the Cross, though the poem says nothing about anything's being on the log. The student says that Christ watches death go through, around, and over him, but in the poem it is the log (the Cross?) that watches these actions. Finally, the writer says that the Son of God is disguised as man; in the poem the log is so disguised. A log so long dead that its heart has rotted and all that remains is a hollow shell seems an unlikely symbol for the Son of God.

A good way to generate discussion about this paper is to ask your students to study the essay carefully and decide whether it is "unsatisfactory," "satisfactory," "good," or "excellent" in its analysis and interpretation of the poem. Have them jot down their evaluations so that their decisions will be firm before you call for a show of hands and record the evaluations on the board. Ask two or three of the students who rated the paper "excellent" (or considered that rating, if no one actually awarded it) to speak very briefly about what is admirable about the paper and to say nothing about its faults. Then ask two or three who rated the essay "unsatisfactory" (or considered that rating) to speak briefly of its weaknesses and to say nothing about its strengths. Explain that no one else (including yourself) will be allowed to speak until these short speeches are finished and that then anyone who can get the floor may speak. You will have to decide, of course, how much you should say in the last part of the discussion.

If your students respond as did those with whom we tested the "Hunting Song" materials, there will be lively, perhaps bitter, disagreement about the quality of the essay. Though a number of our students thought the essay was unsatisfactory as an analysis and interpretation of the poem, others considered it good, and a few thought it excellent. These few praised it as an imaginative piece of writing. One young man who rated the essay as "excellent" criticized "The Detached Interpreter" (pages 294-295) because that interpretation did not tell him anything about "Hunting Song" that he could not have discovered for himself in a close reading of the poem. Some in the class thought his comment was a compliment to "The Detached Interpreter," but he did not intend it to be.

When you emphasize that not all interpretations of a poem or other literary work are necessarily satisfactory, be prepared to be misunderstood. You will have to explain that you do not mean that

126   Teaching with a Purpose

a good piece of writing has only one meaning, that you not only understand but insist that various interpretations can be sound so long as they are supportable by what actually happens in the work. "Symbolism in 'Hunting Song'" explains what the student insists that the poem shall mean, though patterns of evidence in neither the poem nor the New Testament story support the interpretation.

Exercise (pages 301-305)

This exercise is intended to give students intensive experience in prewriting a critical essay that emphasizes interpretation. The questions are designed to focus on troublesome spots and to help students to deal with particular passages before they make up their minds about the poem as a whole. The assumption is that students will try to provide at least tentative answers to the questions before evaluating these answers collectively as a class. The discussion may provide new insights or raise doubts that will require re-evaluation of the tentative answers. Ideally, students should emerge from the cumulative experience with the conviction that they can make a general interpretation of the poem and can support that interpretation by specific references to the text.

Of the two poems, the first is relatively easy and the second much more difficult. Instructors who feel that "The Going Away of Young People" is too difficult for their students may, of course, limit the assignment to "Bears." The decision to choose poems of unequal difficulty and to let students discuss both before writing on one was intended to challenge some students without penalizing others. And although the assignment requires only analysis and interpretation, there is no reason why some students should not go beyond interpretation to evaluation if they so desire.

It is not the function of this Guide to offer final answers to the questions. Certainly an instructor will not accept the Guide's answers if he or she believes there are better ones, just as students are often reluctant to accept an instructor's reading of a poem. But it may be helpful to see how another teacher responds to these questions.

"Bears"

1. Both the diction and the quality of thought surely make it clear that the speaker is not a child but an adult recalling childhood experiences and reflecting on them.

2. Possible sources are toy bears that the child received as presents, stories read or heard about real bears, and bears seen in zoos. (Though Ms. Rich would not have seen television during her childhood, your students may quite reasonably suggest that the child may know about bears through television programs.)

3. In one sense, the child's bears may have been given long ago to some other child. But the questions seem to be nostalgic, associated by the adult speaker with the joys and fears of

childhood. So it is reasonable to say that in another sense the bears, like the child's farm in Dylan Thomas's "Fern Hill," has "forever fled the childless land." "When did I lose you?" may refer not only to the bears but to childhood itself as the speaker looks back nostalgically to those early years: she lost her bears when she grew out of childhood.

4. The narrator may want to hear the sounds of the bears again to experience once more the excitement of childhood marvels. And on another level she may wish to return to a life less complicated and demanding than her adult life.

5. If the narrator owned stuffed bears when she was a child, some other child--a niece or a child whose grandmother bought the discarded bears at Goodwill--may keep them now. In another sense, all children who admire and dream of bears keep them now, endowing them with the qualities that the speaker once attributed to them.

6. One source is pride of ownership (they were "my" bears), supplemented by maternal pride such as a little girl may have because of her dolls--the pride that comes from having something or someone to love and care for. Another source may be the pride that comes from being associated with such special animals as are bears that live in a child's imagination. The fear may have a more complex source--fear of the savagery of real wild bears; fear of losing a valuable possession like the toy bears; fear of being deprived of a satisfying, intimate relationship in which the child's bears serve as security blankets; perhaps even fear of growing up to a time when bears will no longer mean what they used to mean.

"The Going Away of Young People"

Stanza 1

1. The crumbs on the table may be a sign that the routine of the home has been interrupted by the departure of the young person. The mother is too depressed to do normal chores. Her mind is on the one who has gone, not on housekeeping.

2. The darkness is psychological. Even though the room is filled with sunlight, it seems dark because the person who occupied it is not there. She may also associate the darkness that seems to be in the room with those days when the drapes or blinds were closed because the young person was sleeping late.

3. Since it is usual for departing members of a family to forget things during the process of leaving, the mother is probably concerned about finding and mailing anything her young person has forgotten and needs. But the departing person in this stanza has left nothing that is needed except love. The mother's statement that she will mail it is ironic, for the love that is left in the house cannot be mailed, though expressions of that love may be enclosed in letters.

4. A reader may see the string, paper, and other "stuff" as things left over from the packing. Getting rid of such material is a normal part of cleaning up after a departure, but since individual items are now mementos of the young person, the mother will probably save them. Another reader might assume that the mother does not at this moment feel up to the chore of wrapping and tying things to be mailed. Besides, she associates the "stuff" with her love for her child and has learned to feel comfortable with it, even with stumbling over it.

5. While the son or daughter was in the house, the hi-fi was frequently on, but now it is off, and the contrast of the unusual quiet is painful. The two lines about the hi-fi are a distraction that interrupts the mother's thoughts about the forgotten love. The reference to the stringing of the psyche helps explain the less than perfect coherence of the mother's thoughts.

6. She is depressed and saddened, as mothers usually are when their offspring leave home. In a sense the part of her life in which she was most needed, most involved, and most happy is over.

Stanza 2

1. If the sailers-away are construed as those young people who have left homes such as this one, the use of <u>sailers</u> instead of <u>sailors</u> is puzzling. Perhaps <u>-ers</u> is used instead of <u>-ors</u> because the departing young people are not really sailors but people who have sailed away. Here is a different reading: since the "sailers-away" are hanging "full sail" in the windows, perhaps they are curtains blowing, somewhat like sails, in the open "autumn windows." For some readers the image of departing young people and that of blowing curtains may blend together.

2. The garage is unused, the uncut grass is spreading into the flower beds, and the curtains are probably drawn. These details suggest either an unoccupied house or one whose occupants (certainly there are no children there) are isolated within. (The metaphor of the becalmed house likens the house across the street to a ship deprived of the wind and therefore motionless.)

3. Though much of the life has gone out of it, the first house--that is, the house in stanza 1--is still occupied. There is still someone in it who looks through the window and sees, at least in her mind's eye, the young person who has sailed away.

4. The reference to both houses in the same short stanza suggests that the speaker senses a certain similarity between her house and the one across the street that is "becalmed." In later stanzas the feeling that she has to some extent "lost" her young person is strengthened by such statements as "all leave-taking is a permanence" (stanza 3) and "Windows . . . / At last reflect only me" (stanza 5). Even so, she finally retains a ray of hope that the young person may return ("In case you come back"). The whole context of the poem suggests that she thinks her house too will gradually lose its associations with the

young person who went away and to that extent will be "becalmed of young people."

5. The safest assumption seems to be that the speaker in stanza 3 is the same as the one in stanza 1--indeed, that the mother in stanza 1 continues to be the main speaker throughout the poem.

6. Yes. Both houses illustrate a common theme of "The Going Away of Young People."

Stanza 3

1. The statement "I won't say goodbye" is likely to be made at any parting between friends in an attempt to offer assurance that the parting will not be permanent. In this stanza the statement could recall the parting words spoken by any of three people: the young person of stanza 1, the mother in that stanza, or _her_ mother. Perhaps the mother in stanza 1 is recalling the parting words of her young person and remembering that these were the same words she spoke to her mother on a similar occasion.

2. Both _a_ and _b_. Two situations, a generation apart, blend into one, indicating that such partings recur in each generation.

3. Literally, September is the beginning of fall, when vegetation begins to fade. September is also the month in which young people traditionally leave home to enter college. It is possible, though not necessary, to infer that in both generations the "going away" was a departure for college. In any case, the September referred to seems to be one that occurred so long ago that it is faded in memory.

Stanza 4

1. The speaker is offering sympathy partly because of the friend's regret that things have not turned out as she had hoped they would, but perhaps also because the mother in stanza 1 feels that her friend's sense of loss is in some ways similar to her own. (The friend may live in the becalmed house across the street.)

2. Obviously the friend regrets the turn that events have taken and feels that she is somehow to blame for the change. The use of _too_ is particularly interesting. The friend may mean "I, as well as you, have failed." But we must consider that the friend's statement "I've failed, too" follows immediately after she "cuts at the traffic" and says "It was all woods!" The idyllic woods have yielded to the traffic of the streets. Thus she may feel that the woods, which she had counted on to keep her children in an environment safe from harm, have failed.

3. Here, as in other stanzas, there is a feeling of loss and of despondency over that loss.

Stanza 5

1. In the last stanza windows are looking glasses in which the woman can see images of the past, present, and future crowding together into one comprehensive view of the loneliness that the going away of young people leaves behind. Until the last stanza, there has been no suggestion that windows cannot be seen through; in fact, there is some evidence that the windows in line 2 of stanza 2 are open, framing the "sailers-away." (One window in the last stanza is treated differently from the others: the mother opens the window over the young person's bed, hoping that the child will return for the forgotten love.)

2. Perhaps only the mother is left in an empty house; certainly she is alone in what she considers an empty life.

3. Yes. "In case you should come back / For what you forgot" echoes "You forgot your love" of stanza 1. The poem can be said to represent a circle that began when the woman parted from her mother one faded September and ends with her reliving her mother's feelings about that departure. A circle has no end; so perhaps the poem suggests that the going away of young people brings a loss that every mother must endure.

Whatever answers students choose for these questions, their attempts to express them should lead into a closer reading than they are likely to do without the questions and provide them with material for some general interpretation. A major reason for discussing these questions separately and in order is to prevent a hasty interpretation that leaps too suddenly to a conclusion. For this reason the instructor should discourage any evaluative judgment of the poem as a whole until the answers to the questions have been fully discussed. Then students can make judgments if they wish.

Since the experiences being recorded in the poem are those of a mother rather than a young person, college freshmen are likely to be less sensitive to these experiences than their parents, and for that reason some students may judge the poem sentimental, which in a sense it is. They may object to the absence of a father in the poem or to the barrennness of a life that has no existence outside of the parent-child relationship. It may be difficult for them to understand that such objections have no pertinence in a reading of this poem. The poem is what it is, and it is not about the young person's view of leaving home or about father-mother relationships, nor is it about how to adjust to the going away of young people by plunging oneself into social or community activities. In this poem there are no other children and no father, and why does not matter; in this poem there is not, and cannot be, any activity for the mother that will keep her mind off the departure of her child. Perhaps there will be opportunities in the discussion to suggest to students that a poem has to be true only to itself. It should be judged by how well it does what it attempts to do, not by standards that exist outside the poem.

SOME CONCLUDING SUGGESTIONS

Three Elementary Problems

One elementary composition problem that can become particularly troublesome when students write about literature is that of maintaining consistency in verb tense. The critic will probably speak in the present tense about what the author does or what the narrator says: "In 'King of the Bingo Game' Ellison <u>shows</u> . . . ," or "Adrienne Rich <u>suggests</u> in 'Bears' that . . . ," or "Huckleberry <u>says</u> . . . ." The critic may discuss the action of the work using either the present or the past as the basic tense. What the critic must do is to determine what will be the most desirable relationship of verb tenses in the paper and then make choices consistently within that decision.

Another problem common in writing about literature is the mixing of third- and first-person pronouns when a quotation is blended with the student's words:

> After Huckleberry wrote the note telling Miss Watson how she could claim her runaway slave, his conscience was clear and he "knowed I could pray now."

The problem can be solved through paraphrasing:

> . . . his conscience was clear, and he knew that at last he could pray.

Or the student can set up a direct quotation in which the subject of <u>knowed</u> is included in the quotation:

> . . . his conscience was clear. He says, "I knowed I could pray now."

A third problem that often troubles student critics occurs when they quote lines of poetry. You can easily show them two ways to quote correctly. One is to single space, indent, and set the poetic lines up as they appear in the poem, using no quotation marks. (See the <u>MLA Handbook</u>, page 21, if you want that publication's recommendation for setting up lines of poetry in a research paper.) The other method, used only for passages of three lines or less, is to include the quotation in the regular line pattern of the essay, add a spaced slash mark between lines of poetry (maintaining the initial upper- or lower-case style of each line), and use quotation marks. These techniques are elementary to you, but many students do not know about them. Both techniques are used in "The Detached Interpreter" (pages 294-295).

The Poorly Prepared Student

In almost every freshman class there will be at least a few students who feel almost totally incompetent to write critical essays about literature--mainly because they have never done it and haven't the vaguest idea how to go about the job. Quite understandably, insecure students often attempt to solve their problem by summarizing the plot. These students need instruction in the techniques of analysis and practice in making interpretations and judgments. Make your points about literary criticism simply and clearly. It would be easy to overwhelm and frighten such students with a mass of unnecessarily complex information about literary criticism.

Another technique that insecure students use is to rely heavily on what professional critics have said about a work. You should stress that if secondary sources are used, they must be cited. Take a little time to show your students when and how to cite sources, even though they are not writing research papers, or refer them to pages 349-353 in the text.

Literature-related Themes

One of the major problems in freshman courses that concentrate on writing about literature is that students who have little talent for or interest in literary criticism are forced into the role of critic in paper after paper, with no relief. But not all your students' papers that grow out of literature need be papers in literary criticism—that is, they need not all concentrate on analyzing, interpreting, and evaluating the literary work itself. Some of the most interesting writing done by students can be on nonliterary subjects that are suggested by their reading. It is entirely reasonable that this should be true. After all, literature speaks of subjects that matter to us—people's capacity for evil and for good, their fragility and ability to endure, their fears and hopes, their shallowness and emotional depth. Within such general topics students can discover real subjects for their papers. Reading about Reverend Dimmesdale in The Scarlet Letter may lead one student to write about the difficulty people sometimes have in willingly accepting responsibility for their behavior. The story of Wilhelm in Saul Bellows' Seize the Day may cause another to write of the frustration that accompanies unsuccessful attempts to discover one's identity. Reading Lord of the Flies may motivate still another to speculate about the directions human nature takes when people are not held in check by conventional restraints. Such papers would be critical essays insofar as they involved analysis, interpretation, and judgment; but they would not at all be papers in literary criticism.

Importance of Understanding What Happens in the Work

Do not underestimate the value of students' knowing very thoroughly what happens on the literal level in the work being studied. Until they do, they cannot analyze, interpret, or evaluate reasonably. One experienced teacher reports observing a freshman class trying to discuss symbolic values in Conrad's Heart of Darkness. The students were earnestly engaging in such activities as juxtaposing black and white, pondering the significance of ivory, and wondering what symbols could clarify Mr. Kurtz's problem—but doing none of this very clearly. The beginning teacher knew the story well, certainly the book was worth the effort, and the students were interested. Why the lack of competence in discussing the work? The observer says that he finally realized that the students did not yet have a good command of the plot. They did not know precisely what happens on the literal level as Marlow makes his trip into the heart of the Congo to find Kurtz, but they were already searching for symbols. Some teachers call this condition "symbolosis," an affliction to be avoided like the dread disease that it can be for the neophyte student of literature.

Forced Interpretations: Problems with Symbols

The problem of forced interpretations is so common and so major that it deserves final attention here, though it is discussed in both the text (pages 295-296) and earlier in this chapter (see the comments on "Symbolism in 'Hunting Song,'" pages 123-126). Students' "pushing a work around," trying to make it say something it does not say, is one of the most perplexing problems teachers encounter when their students write about literature. The problem is compounded when symbols are involved.

In an earlier edition of Writing with a Purpose McCrimmon speaks of a legitimate kind of interpretation of symbols:

> Writers . . . often use open symbols to invite the reader to make whatever associations that the symbols reasonably suggest. Golding's Lord of the Flies is full of such symbols: the conch that Ralph blows to call the boys to a meeting is a symbol of democratic procedures, the fire is a traditional symbol of civilization in contrast to the barbarism of Jack and his hunters, the dead airman dangling from a parachute in a tree is a symbol both of the destructiveness of war and of the terror the boys associate with the "beast," and the sow's head covered with flies is a symbol of human corruption and of the devil.[1]

But these interpretations are not valid just because a reader arbitrarily assigns them to symbols. They are valid because they fit comfortably into a pattern of symbols that enriches and complements, rather than contradicts, the literal meaning of the work.

Since the meanings the reader draws from the symbol "must be appropriate to the whole context of the work, interpreting symbols requires disciplined, as well as imaginative, reading."[2] The widespread belief that a literary work, especially a poem, means

---

[1]. James M. McCrimmon, Writing with a Purpose, Short Edition (Boston: Houghton Mifflin, 1973), p. 196.

[2]. McCrimmon, p. 196.

whatever the reader sees in it sometimes leads to bizarre interpretations of supposed symbols. The following example can help you illustrate this point to your class. In the decade after Hitler's fall some readers insisted that the eagle in the following poem was symbolic of the former German leader.

The Eagle: A Fragment

He clasps the crag with crooked hands;
Close to the sun in lonely lands,
Ringed with the azure world, he stands.

The wrinkled sea beneath him crawls;
He watches from his mountain walls,
And like a thunderbolt he falls.

Alfred Tennyson

In this interpretation the first stanza describes the warped ("crooked hands") despot in his lonely existence high above the world in his mountain hideaway at Berchtesgaden. The second stanza speaks of his military defeat and his fall from high, secure position ("mountain walls") in 1945. Even if we, as careful readers, should reluctantly concede that Tennyson might have had some prophetic insight into human affairs when he wrote the poem about 1850, we would insist that the eagle's ability to descend "like a thunderbolt" is part of his grace and power and has no relationship to a catastrophic collapse and consequent fall from power.

You may want to use the interpretations of the Golding and Tennyson works to contrast legitimate and illegitimate symbol-seeing. Students need to understand that interpreting symbols competently requires both freedom and restraint: freedom to explore the associations suggested by the symbol, and restraint from accepting those inconsistent with an analysis of the whole work.

CHAPTER 13   THE RESEARCH PAPER

The chapter on writing the research paper is an excellent example of how-to-do-it analysis. All the instruction is practical. It speaks simply and directly about the process through which the student prepares for and does the writing of the research paper, and it presents for study a model of the finished paper.

CLOSE INSTRUCTION OVER AN EXTENDED PERIOD

Two of the reasons many research papers are mediocre or less are that instructors permit students to work without adequate guidance and that students plan and write the papers too quickly. Students need time to do their preliminary study carefully and to back away from a false start, if necessary, and begin again. Too often they find themselves in the predicament of having to carry on with a project that they see they never should have begun. Or perhaps the basic subject is all right, but they discover too late that the approach is wrong. Even if the work goes smoothly from the beginning, the extended period is desirable, for it gives students time to reflect on what they are doing and thus discover the appropriate relation of each part of the paper to the other parts. Planning for the research project should begin early in the term; the instructor should devote class time as needed for dealing with troublesome parts of the project; the work should be submitted in stages for the instructor's evaluation and critique; and conferences between instructor and students should be a requirement, especially early in the project.

PRELIMINARY OVERVIEW OF THE ASSIGNMENT

A good way to begin the research paper assignment is to start with an introductory look at the model paper on pages 355-381. You can ask your students to read the paper carefully and to come to class prepared to discuss the purpose of the paper, the thesis, the outline, the relation of the outline to the text of the paper, and the amount and kinds of evidence by which the main divisions of the outline are developed in the text. They need not bother with the endnotes or bibliography at this stage. The function of this preliminary overview is simply to provide an introductory look at the finished assignment without worrying about technical details that can best be discussed when students are ready for them.

CHOICE OF SUBJECT

Choosing appropriate subjects for research papers is exceptionally important for your students. You will want to confer with them early to help them avoid wasting time by working on subjects that will later have to be abandoned or revised so radically that most of the preliminary work proves useless. The most common problem of this sort is the subject that is too broad or that lacks focus. "Various Influences on the English Language" is not a manageable subject for a freshman research paper; "The Influence of French on English Vocabulary after the Battle of Hastings" is.

Another problem is a subject too complex for the student to master in the period of time allotted to the research project. A paper written on such a subject is almost certain to be sketchy or unclear or both. This point would seem to be self-evident, but most students have not had the experience to steer them away from problems that are obvious to the instructor.

A third problem arises from the selection of a subject that requires materials not readily available to the student. If your students cannot get all their materials locally, talk closely with them about the hazards of relying on others to mail booklets and other materials. Too often students discover that important materials are not available only after they cannot afford to change subjects. The results, of course, are incomplete research projects.

Finally, you should caution students about writing on subjects in which they are emotionally involved. One young man of fundamentalist religious convictions was simply incapable of discussing the Catholic Mass with an open mind; his opposition was too deeply rooted in his emotions. If a student does not feel entirely capable of stepping back and looking at a subject with a considerable degree of detachment, he or she should not choose to write on that subject. In general, highly controversial subjects should be chosen with a great deal of caution, if at all.

In order to help students avoid subjects that are potentially troublesome, some instructors devote a class meeting to examining proposed subjects. At this meeting students write their tentative subjects on the board, and the class examines them to see whether they satisfy the conditions stated on pages 330-331. If a subject is not clear, the class will say so and perhaps ask how the student plans to deal with the subject. As the students participate in this sort of evaluative session, they (1) help each other anticipate and avoid problems and (2) become more competent in seeing and managing problems that arise in their own planning. This sort of session is a valuable supplement to individual conferences between students and instructor.

(Note: a subject so foreign to your own knowledge that you feel unable to evaluate a paper written on it presents a special problem. Though you do not want to be overrestrictive in the students' choice of subjects, and though you can evaluate the clarity and methodology of many papers written on subjects that you are not competent to write on, you should avoid becoming obligated to evaluate a paper that you cannot read competently. It is better to say no to a student's proposal than to allow this situation to develop.)

PLANNING THE CLASS INSTRUCTION

In some courses the research project extends over a period of six weeks or more. This does not mean that six weeks of class time must be devoted to the assignment. Students need time to do their reading and note-taking; and while they are engaged in this work, class time is free for whatever activities the instructor wishes to pursue. But whenever students have reached a state at which discussion of specific problems (concerning thesis, outline, bibliography, and so on) can be profitable, class time should be made available for such discussion. Often young instructors feel an obligation to lecture on these occasions, sometimes repeating instructions already given in the textbook. The most efficient strategy is not to lecture but to use the time to resolve students' difficulties with the textbook or with their own research concerns. In such situations probably a question-answer-discussion format is the best use of class time.

For example, when students are ready to announce their tentative theses, you can conduct a session similar to the one already recommended for discussing subjects. In this session you should ask the class to evaluate each thesis by the criteria established in Chapter 3. (If the class is too large for every thesis to be discussed during class time, be sure that those students who do not present their theses do confer privately with you. This matter is crucial.) And at the right time a class discussion of the exercise on bibliography on pages 338-339 can be helpful. But be sure that the students have written their responses to the exercise problems before the discussion is held. The instructor can participate in such a discussion without choking off student involvement if he or she is a consultant rather than a lecturer during this hour.

THE OUTLINE

Because of the importance of the outline of a research paper, students should understand what the instructor will be looking for in outlines. Perhaps the best way to begin is to ask the class to review the tests for an outline of pages 58-60. Then you can ask students to apply these tests to the outline of the model research paper, before applying them to their own outlines. Since outlines are too lengthy to be written on the board for class examination, each has to be handled by the instructor--preferably in conference, but at least by a written criticism. The critique should focus first on the relations between the main headings and the thesis and then on the relations between the subheadings and the main headings. Whether the outline will finally be in topic or sentence form will depend on the kind of paper being written. Keep in mind that (1) a classification paper can take either form and (2) if the paper is to develop a thesis, a sentence outline gives more guidance to the writer and the reader than does a topic outline. Because the sentence outline is more likely to be used and is often more demanding, that form is given more attention than the topic outline in the chapter on the research paper. But if you want to give your students more experience with topic outlines, you can do so by asking them to rewrite the outline of the model paper as a topic outline.

USING A NUMBER OF SOURCES

The nature of the research project requires the student to examine and use material drawn from a variety of sources. A paper on the origins of American place names could have been written entirely from works by George Stewart, an authority on the subject. But if that had been done, the paper would have been little more than a summary of some of Stewart's work.

To prevent students from depending excessively on one or two sources, some instructors require that at least ten sources be used. This rule of thumb oversimplifies the problem, since it is the student's responsibility to survey the possible sources and draw on all of them that are helpful. But some students will ask, quite understandably, "How many sources should we use?" Perhaps the best answer to that question is a statement like this: "Use as many sources as are necessary to give a reader confidence that you have consulted most of the major works on your subject. The author of the model research paper used thirteen sources. Some of you will use more and some less than that number. There is no hard and fast rule about the number of sources you should use, but it should be enough to satisfy you and your reader that you have made a comprehensive search of the material available on your subject."

Exercise (pages 338-339)

1. Fordin, Hugh. Getting to Know Him: A Biography of Oscar Hammerstein II. New York: Random House, 1977.

2. Manley, Seon, and Susan Belcher. O, Those Extraordinary Women! or The Joys of Literary Lib. Philadelphia: Chilton Book Company, 1972.
   (Since the text gives Company as part of the names of the publishers in problems 2, 5, and 9, students will probably include it in their answers. But if they write those publishers as Chilton, Doubleday, and Crowell, the shortened forms are all right. The MLA Handbook endorses, but does not require, shortened forms of publishers' names.)

3. DeVane, William Clyde. A Browning Handbook. 2nd ed. New York: Appleton-Century-Crofts, 1955.

4. Mill, John Stuart. Examination of Sir William Hamilton's Philosophy. 2 vols. New York: Holt, 1877.

5. Gullason, Thomas A., ed. The Complete Novels of Stephen Crane. Garden City, N. Y.: Doubleday and Company, 1967.

6. Bain, Mildred, and Ervin Lewis, eds. <u>From Freedom to Freedom: African Roots in American Soil, Selected Readings</u>. New York: Random House, 1977.

7. Ibsen, Henrik. <u>The Complete Major Prose Plays of Henrik Ibsen</u>. Trans. Rolf Fjelde. New York: New American Library, 1978.

8. American Humane Association. <u>Animal Books for Children</u>. Denver: 1969.

9. Blackmur, R. P. "The Craft of Herman Melville." In <u>American Literary Essays</u>. Ed. Lewis Leary. New York: Thomas Y. Crowell Company, 1960.

10. "Mardi Gras." <u>Encyclopedia Americana</u>. 1977 ed.

11. Paisey, David. "Learning to Read: Friedrich Gedike's Primer." <u>The British Library Journal</u>, 4 (Autumn 1978), 112-121.

12. McCloskey, Michael. "Nature and Cities." <u>Sierra</u>, Apr. 1978, pp. 14-16.

13. "Rhodesia's Cycle of Futility." <u>Los Angeles Times</u>, 15 Sept. 1978, Part 2, p. 6.

NOTE-TAKING

Once your students have determined their real subjects and are beginning to make notes on their reading, it is important that you check sample note cards as early as is feasible. Inefficient note-taking can lead to unintentional plagiarism, and a check of some twenty notes in sequence can allow you to detect potential difficulties: Are the note cards carefully documented? Do they clearly distinguish, in the students' own words, between direct quotations and summaries? Are the notes longer than they need to be, suggesting that the student has inadequate control over the selection of material being recorded and is dominated by an adherence to the wording of his sources? Do the notes have enough continuity to suggest development of some part of the outline and projected paper, or are they merely scattered bits of information not concerned with a common topic?

WRITING THE PAPER

It is useful to require that the first 500 words of the first draft be handed in as a writing assignment. That sample will be about a third or a quarter of the paper. If students are also required to present an outline for this part of the paper, you can study both the organization of the material and the development of the outline. The things to look for in this sample, in addition to structure, are the introduction, the amount of information used to support each outline heading, evidence that the notes are being composed into discursive paragraphs and not just listed in notelike form, the techniques through which quotations are introduced into the text, the positions of endnote markers, and the notes themselves.

In announcing this assignment it will be helpful to have the class look closely at the first four or five pages of "How American Places Get Their Names," with particular attention to the following:

1. the introduction and the way the quotation from Stewart is introduced (see "Using Quotations Skillfully" below)

2. the way the author leads up to his thesis in the second paragraph

3. the blending of information from the note cards into unified and coherent paragraphs

4. the forms of the endnotes for this part of the paper

Class time spent on this kind of analysis can be a useful demonstration of the composing process that the students themselves will be expected to use.

USING QUOTATIONS SKILLFULLY

As you lead your students in a discussion of the first few pages of the model paper, they should profit from an examination of the quotations, since using quoted material skillfully is a problem for many student writers. Several situations in the first five pages of the paper are worth pointing out:

---In the first paragraph (notes 1 and 2) the leading authority on the subject is quoted to show the scope and nature of the problem being investigated. The writer is careful to name the authority before presenting each of the matters attributed to him.

---Students may be puzzled about the form of the material for note 1. In keeping with the __MLA Handbook__ recommendations for writing long quotations, the lines are double spaced (instead of single spaced), indented ten spaces (instead of five spaces), and are preceded and followed by triple spacing (instead of double spacing). (The quoted material for notes 34 and 45 are in the same form.) This form is primarily intended to make easier the task of the printer who is setting up copy of a manuscript that is to be published. But since few freshman papers are ever submitted for publication, you may decide that your students do not need to be concerned with this form. You will have to decide whether you want your students to follow the MLA recommendations or the form you have been accustomed to.

---The words of the sources for notes 2, 7, 12, and 17 have been blended with the words of the writer of the paper. This blending technique is one that not many of your students will try unless you point it out to them and show how smoothly the writer's words and the words of the sources go together.

--- The decision to quote part of the material for note 12 has solved a problem for the writer. He needs the exact information, and the quantitative material does not readily lend itself to paraphrasing. Rather than paraphrase by deviating from the source only superficially, he has quoted directly.

--- The material for note 16 is a good example of how a paper can profit from the quaintness of the style of a source.

If you decide that enough is to be gained from studying the use of quotations to justify going beyond the first five pages of the paper, here are other matters you can point out:

--- The author of the material for note 31 has expressed his point so aptly that to tamper with his wording would be to risk losing the impact of the information.

--- Particularly good stories are told well and economically in the material for notes 34, 39, and 45. It is better to record these stories as they stand than to rewrite them.

--- Three special techniques for quoting are used in the material for note 39:

   a. Square brackets (not parentheses) enclose interpolated material within a quotation.

   b. Single quotation marks enclose material quoted within material that is itself enclosed by double quotation marks.

   c. Slash marks are written between lines of poetry because the lines are written as part of the running manuscript.

AVOIDING PLAGIARISM

The general cause of plagiarism is student ignorance of how research writing is done. The best way to maintain that ignorance is to assume that, having read Chapter 13, students can handle the research project on their own, without periodic checking by the instructor. If you will keep in touch with your students' progress by checking outlines, sample note cards, and a major unit of the writing, you will be able to detect weaknesses early and thus help students to remove them before the final copy is written. Unless you make these checks, some plagiarism is almost certain to occur. You should of course emphasize the section "When to Document" on page 349 in the text.

The most common specific causes of plagiarism are the following:

1. Failure to distinguish between direct quotation and student summary in the note cards. Sometimes a direct quotation is

written on the note card without quotation marks, sometimes a card is a summary of the source, and sometimes a card contains a combination of these kinds of notes; later the student cannot tell one kind of note from the other.

2. The mistaken assumption that as long as a paragraph is cited in an endnote, students are entitled to use both the information and the wording of the source as their own work. This assumption can lead to a paper that is no more than a collection of paragraphs, each of which is taken directly from a source.

3. The assumption that if students paraphrase the content of a source they are justified in claiming it as their own work without endnote citation.

4. The assumption that any change in the wording of a source--even occasional, trivial changes in wording and sentence structure--frees a student to use the material as his or her own. For some students, expressing ideas from a source in their own words amounts to no more than changing a few words in a paragraph. These students have to be taught to extract the information in condensed note form and then to rewrite the passage that is to appear in the paper from the notes, not from the text of the source.

ALTERNATIVES TO THE FULL-SCALE RESEARCH PAPER

Obviously the recommendations that teachers supervise research projects closely and that the work extend over a major portion of the term are central to this chapter in the Guide. But some teachers may respond to the recommendations like this: "All this is fine for the instructor whose classes are small and whose syllabus will permit the students to spread their research projects over a large portion of the term, but neither of these situations is mine. Is there an alternative?" Yes--the documented essay.

As the term documented essay is used here, it refers to a paper approximately five pages long based on about four to six sources. Its scope is likely to be less extensive than that of the longer paper, and the challenge of assimilating information is not so great as when more sources are used. But the documented essay does require the basic skills that the research paper requires: choosing a satisfactory subject for the nature of the assignment and length of the paper, taking notes, arriving at a reasonable thesis, writing an outline, writing from notes, and documenting information. In fact the requirements of the documented essay are so nearly those of the research paper that some teachers have found that students who write the documented essay one term and go the next term into classes where the full research paper is required move easily into the more demanding assignment.

This project is preferable to the full-research paper assignment if teaching conditions will not permit the complete research project to be developed as it should be.

CHAPTER 14   THE BUSINESS LETTER

As the opening paragraph of this chapter points out, the writing of a business letter is a practical application of the principles of effective composition. Students are likely to think that the main concern in writing a business letter is following the conventional forms of inside address, salutation, complimentary close, and so on. But the chief emphasis in this chapter is on the same criteria that defined purpose in Chapter 1: what has to be said and how it is to be said.

Although the main types of business letters are discussed and illustrated, more than half of the chapter is devoted to the important letter of application for a job. Both the discussion and the illustrative models are realistic. McCrimmon assumes that most freshmen will have limited education and experience credentials and therefore will have to do the best they can with what they have; there is no sense in asking them to follow models that assume a college degree and considerable experience in business or industry.

Exercise A (pages 394-395)

This letter is intended as a model of how not to write a letter of application. The content is inadequate and the tone is objectionable. If your students have read the advice presented in the text, they will have no trouble identifying the major faults of the letter.

First, the lead is unconvincing. The writer claims to have spent months investigating different firms before deciding to apply to this one, but evidently all he has learned from his investigations is that there is a "place" for him in this organization. What kind of place does he have in mind, and does the second paragraph suggest that no such place existed in the other firms he investigated? The whole lead is too general and vague to be convincing.

Second, the letter fails completely to offer a potential employer any detailed picture of the applicant's education and experience. The lack of experience is understandable, since the writer admits that he has "not yet had any job," but what excuse is there for the failure to support the excessive claims that he has studied "every phase of economics" and feels "well prepared" for whatever job the company wishes to fill? What courses did he take while he was majoring in economics? What books did he read for these courses? What specifically was the "stress on foreign trade"? What are the talents and skills that make him so confident? The whole application consists of a series of unsupported judgments that no employer could accept without considerable evidence that the judgments were justified by the facts of the young man's education. A data sheet providing detailed information about that education would be more convincing than the boastful generalities of the letter.

Third, the applicant offers no actual references. He says "the college officials" will recommend him, but he does not identify these officials, nor does he state why he knows they will recommend him. To whom is the prospective employer supposed to write--to some unnamed officials in an unnamed college? In the unlikely event that an employer would desire to consult these officials, the applicant's failure to give complete information would frustrate that desire.

HANDBOOK OF GRAMMAR AND USAGE

SENTENCE STRUCTURE

S 1 Review of Sentence Elements

Basic Elements (page 406)

```
       S    V   O       S   V
1. They tried it and it worked.

       S     V   O    S  V       C
2. Nobody likes her; she is too sarcastic.

                      C
3. That dog looks vicious.

           S                            O
4. Those who trust you will not need an explanation.

                O                      O
5. I doubt that he will go, but I'll ask him.

        S    O
6. Did you get the tickets?

           S            C
7. Part of the sentence is illegible.

       V        O
8. They paid you a compliment.

              S                C
9. The trouble with Bill is that he is too sensitive.

                         O
10. We discovered that it was our fault.
```

145

146   Teaching with a Purpose

Subordinate Clauses (pages 407-408)

1. I will do (whatever you say).
                   O

2. (What he told me) is none of your business.
     S

3. The book (that I bought) cost eight dollars.
                M

4. The man (who is wearing the plaid shirt) is his uncle.
            M

5. (If that is how you feel,) why don't you leave?
     M

6. The people (who lived in that house) moved to Minnesota.
            M

7. He said (that he was terribly embarrassed).
            O

8. This is the book (that I want).
            M

9. I would like to know (why they did it).
            O

10. (When you are ready,) call me.
      M

Verbals (page 409)

1. <u>to tell</u>: infinitive, used as object
2. <u>thrilling</u>: participle, used as modifier
3. <u>reading</u>: gerund, used as object
4. <u>to play</u>: infinitive, used as subject
5. <u>drunken</u>: participle, used as modifier
6. <u>disappointed</u>: participle, used as modifier
7. <u>screeching</u>: participle, used as modifier
   <u>jarring</u>: participle, used as modifier
8. <u>thinking</u>: gerund, used as object
9. <u>to have invited</u>: infinitive, used as subject
10. <u>feeling</u>: gerund, used as subject

S 2 Period Fault and Sentence Fragments (page 410)

1. . . . one ambition, to play . . . .
2. . . . this far, we must . . . .
3. . . . the whole audience, not just . . . .
4. . . . with much difficulty, slipping . . . .
5. . . . the top twenty, we forgot . . . .

6. I believe our new member of Congress will successfully meet whatever challenge . . . .
7. . . . a stand," I began . . . .

S 3 Fused Sentences (page 411)

1. . . . in the play-offs. When the game . . . .
2. . . . this matter. There is . . . .
3. . . . must be investigated. Unless better food . . . .
4. . . . when we punctuate. We use . . . .

or

. . . what we mean. When we punctuate . . . .
5. . . . to be helpful. In the last half . . . .
6. . . . in such a way. That is . . . .
7. . . . will refuse it? What do you hope to gain?

or

. . . such an offer? If you know . . . .

S 4 Run-on Sentences (page 412)

1. Because I was not sure which flight Jim would arrive on, I met all the planes coming in from Atlanta. When he was on none of them, I decided that I was wrong about which day he was coming.

2. Since we both object to being misled, we should be able to find a common ground for agreement.

3. After examining all reasonable transportation possibilities, I concluded that indeed I was stranded. I called my professor whose exam I was to take next day and told her that I would probably be absent. Then I started to hitchhike back to school.

4. Interested in learning about Thomas Wolfe's method of writing autobiographical fiction, I read his first novel and then the section of the Nowell biography dealing with his early life. The comparison was fascinating.

5. John Malcolm Brinnin wrote a book called Dylan Thomas in America, of which Mrs. Thomas disapproved. She insisted that a statement from her expressing her disapproval should appear at the beginning of the book.

6. When our freshman writing instructor told us about various theories for teaching writing, we asked him what scholarly research had to say about the matter. After explaining the difficulty of conducting research on the subject, he said, "There's not much that is conclusive."

148 Teaching with a Purpose

S 5 Comma Splice (page 414)

Only one answer for each problem is given below. The period can replace the semicolon or vice versa. The writer will decide which to use, according to the desired degree of separation of the main clauses. Also, the writer can restructure the sentence by subordinating one of the present main clauses to the other.

1. . . . late tonight. Coach . . . .
2. . . . the reader; it is . . . .
3. . . . it today. All you . . . .
4. . . . a professional meeting. Moreover, he . . . .
5. . . . at the time. Looking back . . . .
6. Pay attention; before you . . . .
7. . . . Luke's integrity; strange as it now seems, we . . . .
8. . . . to the Senate; because it . . . .
9. . . . emergency meeting. Although there were others . . . .
10. . . . wasn't; enjoying their memories . . . .

S 6 Faulty Parallelism (page 416)

1. In high school we were asked to write legibly and accurately.

2. The evangelist ended the sermon with a hymn and a call for sinners to repent.

3. Sentence elements that perform parallel functions but are not written in parallel grammatical form should be revised.

4. The article cites three main causes for the energy crisis: the greatly increased demand for oil in industrialized countries, the failure of the big oil companies to build new refineries to meet this demand, and the influence of an increasingly unstable political situation on the supply of oil.

5. The narrator in Invisible Man was idealistic, intelligent, and active in advancing the cause of black people.

   or

   The narrator of Invisible Man was idealistic and intelligent, and he tried to advance the cause of black people.

6. By studying newspaper files and magazine articles and by interviewing knowledgeable people, I was able to gather the information I needed.

7. The executives of a corporation must be concerned with keeping the price of their product competitive and with making a reasonable profit for the stockholders.

8. In President Carter's first two years in office, his main challenges were to persuade Israel and the Arab nations to reach a peace agreement and to find a way to control inflation in the United States.

9. Manipulative commercials encourage people to want things they do not need and to buy things they cannot afford.

10. Because he has always had both wealth and indulgent parents, he has never been forced to accept responsibility.

S 7 Dangling Modifiers (page 418)

1. Although I worked steadily each day, time ran out before I could complete the job.

2. The committee requires that candidates have perfect attendance to qualify for the award.

3. When I was a senior in high school, my English teacher had so many students that he was not able to give close attention to individual students' writing problems.

4. Having heard the weather report, we postponed our trip.

5. If the story is told in the first person, the reader is more likely to grant the narrator's credibility.

6. In order to study the effect of exercise on pigs' hearts, scientists are having pigs jog up to five miles.

7. Because I have quoted two authoritative sources, my reader should realize that my information is trustworthy.

8. Chaucer's work became more meaningful to us as we studied about life in the Middle Ages.

9. Secure in the knowledge that we had finally arrived safely, we welcomed a good night's sleep.

10. Just as I heard a sharp click, the suds subsided and the dial on the top of the washing machine read "drain."

S 8 Shifts in Subjects and Verbs
Shifts in Person and Number (page 419)

1. When you get through a three-hour examination, you are exhausted.
   (A consistent use of third-person pronouns would also be acceptable.)

   or

   Taking a three-hour examination exhausts a person.

2. I tried to learn quadratic equations, but there is a limit to how much math I can learn.

150   Teaching with a Purpose

3. In a situation like that, so many things can happen that we cannot foresee them all. All we can do is decide on a plan and then make whatever changes we have to.
(A consistent use of you or one would also be acceptable.)

4. Loyalty means having complete confidence in someone, even if that person is under suspicion.

5. The book says the battle took place in 1847, but the book is wrong.

Shifts in Subject (page 420)

1.   Students stop worrying about entrance examinations before they depart for the campus. They spend the last days shopping for clothes during the day and partying with friends at night. They give their families little attention, and they no longer think of entrance examinations.

2.   I often have difficulty writing the first draft of a paper. I have trouble finding a main idea to write about, and so face a blank page with a blank mind. When I do think of possible topics, I can't work them out. After writing a few sentences or a paragraph, I have nothing more to say; so I begin to fill up the wastepaper basket with discarded sheets. Thus I show a lack of concentration, the main weakness in my writing.

Shifts in Forms of Verbs (page 421)

1. The more we learned about the proposal, the clearer the issues became.

2. We spent the whole class hour discussing that question, but we arrived at no agreement.

3. I wrote inviting her to the party, but I have received no answer.

4. When we discussed the problem in class, it became quite simple.

5. As Douglas talked, I reminded myself that we would have to reserve judgment about him but that he would have to prove himself.

6. One behavioral scientist has said that he believes permissiveness in the schools leads to student contempt for the schools.

7. Professor Wallingford said that she would return our papers at the next class session.

   or

   Professor Wallingford said, "I will return your papers at the next class session."

8. The rescue party worked for hours to extricate the child from the wreckage, and finally they succeeded.

9. He said we would be late for class anyway, so we should finish our Cokes and not worry.

    or

    He said, "We'll be late for class anyway; so let's finish our Cokes and not worry."

10. In choosing a mate for the rest of your life, you should look for certain qualities.

S 9 Incomplete Constructions (page 423)

1. We studied the subject as carefully as our opposition did.

2. I question the premise on which the argument depends.

    or

    I question the premise which the argument depends on.

3. I scribbled and outlined until I had exhausted my imagination, but I produced no satisfactory result.

4. Jason Compson, in The Sound and the Fury, is one of the most despicable characters in all of Faulkner's fiction.

    or

    Jason Compson, in The Sound and the Fury, is at least as despicable as any character in all of Faulkner's fiction.

    or

    Jason Compson, in The Sound and the Fury, may be the most despicable character in all of Faulkner's fiction.

5. Senator Benson has spoken more convincingly against the denial of civil rights than his opponent has.

6. We have insisted, and will continue to insist throughout the campaign, on equal opportunity for every ethnic group.

7. I sometimes think our professor has a better understanding of Macbeth than Shakespeare had.

8. One of the most valuable recommendations that the steering committee received came from a housewife whom the committee chairman inadvertently failed to mention.
   (Other revisions are possible. See 4 above.)

152   Teaching with a Purpose

9. Our expectation is that the proposal will be rejected at the polls.

10. In the last quarter State launched a furious passing attack and won its fifth straight victory.

DICTION

D 1 Using a Dictionary (pages 426-427)

   This exercise can provide the basis for an interesting class discussion if you will ask your students to bring their dictionaries to class on the day you work with it. The exercise itself will not require much class time, for the students will have learned, as they answered the questions, what the exercise is intended to teach. Item 4 can lead into other questions that you raise and that the students respond to as they check their dictionaries. The purposes of this part of the session will be to (1) help the students become still more knowledgeable about how to use dictionaries and (2) show them that even very good dictionaries have significant differences. This second purpose need not be a source of confusion: as the students learn about inconsistencies, they should discard naive ideas about what the dictionary says.

   In the material below, the most recent versions of three desk dictionaries will be cited: The American Heritage Dictionary of the English Language (AH), Webster's New Collegiate Dictionary (WNC), and Webster's New World Dictionary of the American Language (WNW). The information from these three widely used dictionaries will help you to anticipate the kinds of responses that will emerge in class discussion. (The first item below is related to item 4 in the exercise.)

   Order of definitions   Some students become confused when the first definition is not the one they need, for they do not know that some dictionaries (including WNC and WNW) list definitions from earliest to most recent meanings. But not all dictionaries do that; for example, the editors of AH have tried to present meanings in "psychologically meaningful order, with one subgroup leading into another" (page xlvi). If you ask your students to turn to shambles in their dictionaries, you can make the point about order of definitions. Here are what WNC, WNW, and AH give:

WNC: 1. archaic : a meat market   2 : SLAUGHTERHOUSE   3a : a place of mass slaughter or bloodshed   b : a scene or a state of great destruction: WRECKAGE   c : a state of great disorder or confusion

WNW: 1. [Archaic exc. Brit. Dial.] a place where meat is sold; butcher's stall or shop   2. a slaughterhouse   3. scene of great slaughter, bloodshed, or carnage   4. any scene or condition of great destruction or disorder [rooms left a shambles by conventioneers]

AH: 1. A scene or condition of complete disorder or ruin: <u>The brawlers left the bar in a shambles.</u> . . . 2. A place or scene of bloodshed or carnage. 3. A slaughterhouse. 4. <u>British</u>. A meat market or butcher shop. . . .

<u>Spelling</u> If you will ask your students to locate the following words in their dictionaries, an informative discussion about spelling can develop. They can begin to develop criteria for determining whether a particular spelling is appropriate in their writing.

<u>judgment</u>: In <u>WNC</u>, <u>WNW</u>, and <u>AH</u>, <u>judgment</u> is listed first and <u>judgement</u> second. There is no notation about the <u>e</u>'s being primarily British. A student need not be troubled, then, by whether to include or omit the <u>e</u>, as long as the same spelling is used throughout the paper.

<u>benefited</u>, <u>benefiting</u>: <u>WNC</u> spells these words with both the single and the double <u>t</u>; neither <u>WNW</u> nor <u>AH</u> gives the double <u>t</u> spellings. You can explain that the double <u>t</u> spelling has come into usage because in so many verbs the final consonant is doubled before a suffix beginning with a vowel: <u>stopped</u>, <u>committed</u>, <u>controlled</u>. Such verbs normally are either one-syllable words or words of more than one syllable with the accent on the final syllable. (See page 495 in the text for more complete information.)

<u>alright</u>: <u>WNC</u> merely lists <u>alright</u> as another spelling for <u>all right</u>, with no comment. <u>WNW</u> says, "a disputed var. sp. of <u>all right</u>." <u>AH</u> says, "a common misspelling." The student is well advised to use <u>all right</u>, but an instructor should be slow to condemn <u>alright</u> severely. (If you can take an old dictionary to class, you can show that <u>alright</u> is not listed in it. The students may enjoy speculating about whether all dictionaries will accept the spelling one or two decades from now.)

<u>alot</u>: None of the three dictionaries lists this widely used misspelling. This sort of evidence should warn the student against its use.

<u>Usage and usage labels</u> The following quotations about criteria for determining acceptable usage show that the three dictionaries take similar, but by no means identical, stances on the subject of usage.

<u>WNC</u>: Three types of status labels are used in this dictionary--temporal, regional, and stylistic--to signal that a word or a sense of a word is not part of the standard vocabulary of English (page 15a).

<u>WNW</u>: . . . usage varies among groups of people, according to locality, level of education, social environment, etc. . . . usage varies for an individual in any given day depending upon the particular situation . . . and the purpose his language must serve. . . . None of the modes of using language in the cases cited is in an absolute sense more correct than

any of the others. Each is right for its occasion . . . (page xiii).

AH: The makers of [this dictionary] accept usage as the authority for correctness, but they have eschewed the "scientific" delusion that a dictionary should contain no value judgments. . . . good usage can usually be distinguished from bad usage . . . . The best authorities, at least for cultivated usage, are those professional speakers and writers who have demonstrated their sensitiveness to the language and their power to wield it effectively and beautifully (page xxiii).

Though there are some differences in temporal and regional labels, the similarities are conspicuous: all use obsolete, archaic, dialect or regional, and British.

But the stylistic usage labels, the ones that are most important to writers, are interesting because of their differences. WNW does not list nonstandard; AH and WNC do, but with quite different meanings (see page xliv in AH and page 16a in WNC). WNC is the only one of the three to use substandard as a label (16a), though WNW uses the term in explanatory notes. AH is the only one to use informal (xliv) and vulgar (xlv). Only WNW uses colloquial (xiv). But all three use the label slang (xliv-xlv in AH, 16a in WNC, xiv in WNW).

Here are some words that the three dictionaries label differently. Ask your students to see what their dictionaries say about them. (You may as well begin with ain't, for the students are going to mention it anyway. All three dictionaries contain discussions of ain't; the one in AH is rather lengthy.)

ain't

WNC: substandard when used to mean have not or has not
WNW: colloquial for am not; dialectal or substandard when it means is not, are not, has not, or have not
AH: nonstandard (see the usage note)

nowheres

WNC: chiefly dialect
WNW: dialect or colloquial
AH: nonstandard

irregardless

WNC: nonstandard
WNW: (no label--explanatory note that it is substandard or humorous)
AH: nonstandard (But remember that nonstandard does not have the same meaning in AH and WNC.)

Class discussion of matters relevant to the material presented here should convince the student that (1) he or she must become well acquainted with the particular dictionary being used in order to get full service from it and (2) there is no point in speaking of what <u>the</u> dictionary says on controversial matters about language as if there were only one correct answer to any particular question.

WORD ORDER

WO 2 Ambiguous Order (pages 432-433)

1. My mother planted in her garden the rosebush that I gave her on Mother's Day.

2. The children watched with shining eyes while the magician drew out a rabbit.

3. No boy, unless he was spiteful, would treat his father like that.

4. The list of expenses tells quickly and clearly the story of the man who wrote it.

·5. Tonight in the student lounge there is a panel discussion about drug addiction.

6. Bill promised to pick me up on his way home.

7. When I met her I was so surprised that I forgot what I intended to say to her.

8. His neighbors said that at one time he had been in jail.

9. Richard Burton played superbly the part of the man who was corrupted by power.

10. There was a noisy disturbance at the back of the hall when the speaker said that.

11. The car that he wrecked is in the garage.

12. They talked frequently about going on a second honeymoon but never did.

WO 4 Unemphatic Order (page 435)

1. In the coroner's judgment, the cause of death was not drowning but heart failure.

2. Even her parents do not know where she is.

3. The challenger shocked the crowd when he knocked down the champion six times in two rounds.

4. Although the plane's tires had been riddled by FBI marksmen who were there to prevent a hijacking, it made a successful take-off.

5. According to the late news last night, the Supreme Court refused to consider the appeal.

6. I think Wayne's personality will irritate other members of the council; however, I'll have to vote for him.

7. Since there was no objection to the minutes, the chairman said they would be accepted.

8. I firmly believe that the best argument for democracy is to consider its alternatives.

9. After much pleading from the students, the instructor promised that she would give the class some sample questions to study for the exam.

10. If you will examine the evidence carefully and impartially, you will see that it shows that the National League plays the best baseball.

11. I neither support nor oppose the bill.

GRAMMATICAL FORMS

GF 1 Principal Parts of Verbs (page 440)

1. lay
2. raise
3. raise
4. sit
5. rose
6. lying
7. lay
8. setting
9. raised
10. lying

GF 2 Tense Forms (page 443)

1. had planned
2. OK
3. Having practiced
4. had had
5. to pack
6. Two possibilities: either change is lucky to was lucky or change to find to to have found
7. had sensed
8. having finished
9. to submit
10. went . . . had intended

GF 3 Case (page 447)

1. OK
2. OK
3. we . . . OK
4. I
5. OK
6. our
7. OK
8. OK
9. whom
10. us . . . me
11. whoever
12. OK

GF 4 Subject-Verb Agreement (pages 453-454)

1. were   6. are
2. plans   7. is
3. was   8. is
4. has   9. is
5. plan   10. are

GF 5 Pronoun-Antecedent Agreement (page 457)

1. his   6. its
2. himself or herself   7. is . . . its
3. one has   8. his or her
4. its . . . it   9. who
5. that   10. they want

GF 6 Vague Pronoun Reference (page 458)

   The sentences can of course be revised in various ways. In several of the solutions below the writer has merely removed the vague pronoun and substituted its understood referent.

  1. The defendant was visibly upset. At that very moment the jurors were in the next room deciding his fate.

  2. Our having overspent our budget for the play is a major problem, for we need still more money for props and set construction.

  3. In revival meetings it is customary for the worshipers to offer testimonies.

  4. Hunters should be careful about how they carry loaded guns.

  5. Because Mark Twain did not like his early work on <u>Huckleberry Finn</u>, he considered destroying the partially completed manuscript.

  6. The figure skaters anxiously awaited the decision as the judges tabulated their score cards.

  7. That Fred and Sue have agreed to have a church wedding pleases their parents.

  8. My mother was pleased because my job in New York was only three blocks from my apartment and because the working hours were during the daytime.

  9. Kemper's sketches of birds and trees showed where his interests lay.

 10. Students living in an apartment will spend some of their time doing their own cooking and cleaning.

158 Teaching with a Purpose

GF 7 <u>Faulty Complement</u> (page 461)

Alternate solutions to several of the problems would be entirely acceptable.

1. My only preparation for college chemistry was a junior high school course in general science.

2. I feel bad about having caused you so much trouble.

3. Forgery is the offense of signing another person's name to a document.

4. I heard on last night's news that flooding has reached disaster proportions in some sections of the country.

5. In basketball, goal tending is the act of blocking an opponent's shot after it has begun its downward path toward the goal.

6. We reached complete accord in our conference.

7. The most unusual food I have ever eaten was a serving of boiled snails.

8. In tennis a double fault occurs when the server fails twice successively to hit the ball into the appropriate part of the opponent's court.

9. The boxer's chief disadvantage is that his opponents have learned that he has a "glass chin."

10. The judge explained that perjury is the crime of lying under oath.

GF 8 <u>Confusion of Adjective and Adverb</u> (page 462)

1. gently
2. surely
3. horrible
4. securely
5. calmly
6. really
7. happy
8. safe
9. carefully
10. considerably

PUNCTUATION

P 1 <u>Uses of the Comma</u>

<u>Commas to Separate Elements</u> (page 467)

1. The largest city in the world is Jacksonville, Florida, if you judge by area, not population.

2. I'll have orange juice, waffles with maple syrup, and black coffee.

3. When we finished sanding and staining, the desk looked beautiful.

4. "But the name is Manson, not Mason," said Aunt Lois.

5. After all, it was not such a difficult shot for a professional.

6. The yard was strewn with empty cartons, newspapers, scraps of lumber, and discarded tires.

7. Throughout, his speech was a masterful exhibition of how to talk around a question without answering it.

8. Father went to the airport to meet his sister, and Mother came with me to the reception.

9. Lyndon Baines Johnson, thirty-sixth President of the United States, was born near Stonewall, Texas, on August 27, 1908, and died on January 22, 1973.

10. No, I cannot wait any longer, for the train leaves in ten minutes.

Commas to Set Off an Interrupting Construction (pages 471-472)

1. Dad, did you know that Dr. Jones, our chemistry professor, once played professional hockey?

2. Mary asked, "Joe, why don't you talk to the man in charge, the managing editor?"

3. Yes, her mother is a doctor--not, however, of medicine, but of philosophy.

4. No commas required.

5. The man, whoever he is, must be found.

6. No commas required.

7. Fred asked me, when he called last night, if we were still going to have the picnic. (In a particular context "when he called last night" might be restrictive and would therefore not be set off by commas.)

8. The children, looking very disappointed, thanked us anyway.

9. The instructor said, in addition, that some of the test answers were illegible.

10. No commas required.

11. Dad, you said we could go if we had finished our work. You promised, moreover, that we could use the car, even though the direction signal is not working.

160   Teaching with a Purpose

12. A radio report, which may or may not be true, states that John Whalen, our line coach, has an offer from a professional team that he will probably accept.

13. The challenger, who was clearly the underdog before the match, made his defeat of the champion look so easy that the sportswriters began to hail him as one of the truly great champions.

14. However, the wig that she bought in the bargain basement was the best of the three.

15. The bus driver, Mr. Peterson, who is usually an easygoing person, was in a bad mood today, scolding the children at the slightest provocation.

Commas to Mark an Inversion (page 473)

1. Whatever he says, take it with a grain of salt.

2. No commas required.

3. If he is going to fly off the handle like that at the slightest provocation, I think you should stop dating him.

4. As far as I know, they plan to stay here this summer.

5. Whatever the merits of the proposal, it comes too late to be considered.

6. Whether you like it or not, this is the final decision.

7. No commas required.

8. Since he has not answered any of our letters, even those we sent by registered mail, we must assume that he is not interested.

9. Knowing that his only chance to win might depend on stealing second base, the manager sent in a runner for Milney.

10. Confused and hurt by her parents' attitude, the girl ran sobbing to her room.

Review Exercise in Punctuation (pages 487-488)

1. Mr. Reynolds, the insurance agent, had not arrived by nine o'clock.

2. "I wonder what's keeping him," Dad grumbled. "Are you sure that he said he would call at eight o'clock?"

3. "Yes, quite sure," I replied. He said to me, "Tell your father I will call at eight o'clock."

4. I have not seen Mrs. Manlin for some time; since her husband was killed she spends a lot of time at her mother's place.

5. Gutenberg, the inventor of movable type, was motivated by a desire to make the Bible more widely available.

6. OK

7. The speaker, who was obviously embarrassed, said that he did not answer questions of such a personal nature.

8. No wonder her hair looks different; she's wearing a wig.

9. Some of the shutters had fallen to the ground, others were hanging from one corner, and a few were firmly locked in place across the windows.

10. Seated at the speakers' table were Fred Hanley, Superintendent of Schools; Dr. Mason, Dean of the College of Education; Mrs. Helen Loftus, President of the Parent Teachers Association; and the chairman, Professor Robbins.

11. The girl who received first prize, a silver cup, was our neighbors' daughter.

12. OK

13. However important these facts may have been eight years ago, they have no significance today.

14. Trevino, despite the pressure he was under, continued to joke with the gallery.

15. He said, when I asked him, that he expected to take a brief vacation.

16. She said, "When I asked his opinion, he answered, 'If you want legal advice, I'll be glad to talk with you in my office.'"

17. Donald said, if I remember correctly, that he would be out of town for the next three or four days.

18. Where the old ice house used to be, there is now a little stone cottage with a white picket fence around it.

19. Giggling almost hysterically, the children either could not or would not explain what had happened.

20. Mules, though less speedy than horses in open country, are both faster and surer on those narrow mountain tracks.

162 Teaching with a Purpose

Review Exercise in Punctuation (pages 488-489)

The punctuation provided here is that of the Newsweek story from which the passage was taken. Alternative punctuation would be possible at some points.

> The plight of a normal person who finds himself committed to a mental institution and unable to convince anyone he is not insane is a standard plot for horror fiction. But in a remarkable study last week, Dr. David L. Rosenhan, professor of psychology and law at Stanford University, and seven associates reported just such a nightmare in real life. To find out how well psychiatric professionals can distinguish the normal from the sick, they had themselves committed to mental institutions. Their experiment, reported in the journal Science, clearly showed that once inside the hospital walls, everyone is judged insane.
> The "pseudopatients,"[1] five men and three women, included three psychologists, a pediatrician, a psychiatrist, a painter and a housewife, all of whom were certifiably sane. In the course of the three-year study, the volunteers spent an average of nineteen days in a dozen institutions, private and public, in New York, California, Pennsylvania, Oregon and Delaware. Each pseudopatient told admitting doctors that he kept hearing voices that said words like "empty," "hollow" and "void," suggesting that the patient found his life meaningless and futile. But beyond falsifying their names and occupations, all the volunteers described their life histories as they actually were. In so doing, they gave the doctors every chance to discern the truth. "I couldn't believe we wouldn't be found out," Rosenhan told Newsweek's Gerald Lubenow. But they weren't. At eleven hospitals the pseudopatients were promptly diagnosed as schizophrenic and, at the twelfth, as manic-depressive.
> As soon as they had gained admission, the volunteers studiously resumed normal behavior. They denied hearing voices and worked hard to convince the staff members that they ought to be released. But such efforts were to no avail; doctors and nurses interpreted everything the pseudopatients did in terms of the original diagnosis. When some of the volunteers went about taking notes, the hospital staff made such entries in their records as "patient engages in writing behavior." The only people who realized that the experimenters were normal were

---

1. Note that the writers follow Newsweek policy of writing a coined word within quotation marks the first time it appears in the article, but not afterwards.

some of the patients. "You're not crazy," said one
patient. "You're a journalist or a professor.
You're checking up on the hospital." (Copyright
Newsweek, Inc., 1973, reprinted by permission.)

MECHANICS

In this section, while you are discussing spelling difficulties and methods of improvement, it might be helpful to emphasize to students the usefulness of the two lists of words frequently confused or misspelled (pages 495, 496-500). Here they are collected for convenient reference when a student is in doubt about their spelling.

Review Exercise in Mechanics (pages 510-511)

1. Dr. Lindon . . . professor . . . University . . . .

2. Columbus discovered America in A.D. 1492 (or 1492 A.D.).

3. Four days . . . .

4. Her father is a lieutenant colonel in the Army of the United States.

5. Lower case spelling for senior, sophomores, juniors, and instructor's. Freshman is capitalized only because it begins a sentence.

6. Capitalize Father's Day.

7. Small n in navy.

8. . . . five days

9. . . . "Spotted Horses," . . . The Hamlet.

10. Capitalize New Year's Day.

11. . . . 71 Grand Ave. (or Avenue.)

12. No capital for mother-in-law.

13. . . . January 31 at 11:05 P.M. (or p.m.)

14. No correction needed.

15. . . . Bible . . . Biblical scholars.

16. Seventy-eight . . . .

17. Italicize pas de deux and tour jeté.

18. Italicize, or put quotation marks around, concave and convex.

19. Capitalize *American* and *European*. Italicize the titles of all these movies.

20. Capitalize *Democratic*, *Vice Presidents*, *Presidency*, *President*, *Chief Executive*, *Presidents*.

BIBLIOGRAPHY

The following works form a selective bibliography for teachers of composition. The headings should contribute to the usefulness of the bibliography. Some of the works could, of course, be listed under more than one heading.

GENERAL

Allen, Harold B., ed. Readings in Applied English Linguistics. 2nd ed. New York: Appleton-Century-Crofts, 1964. An anthology of essays on linguistics and the application of linguistics to the teaching of composition and literature. A good introductory cross-section of the work being done in language by serious scholars.

Corbett, Edward P. J., and Gary Tate, eds. Teaching Freshman Composition. New York: Oxford Univ. Press, 1967. A collection of thirty essays on the teaching of writing. Organized under the headings "General Surveys," "The Literary Approach to Composition," "The Linguistic Approach to Composition," "The Rhetorical Approach to Composition," "Theme Assignments and Evaluation," "Stylistics and Composition," and "Attitudes."

Gorrell, Robert M. "Freshman Composition." In The College Teaching of English, ed. John C. Gerber. New York: Appleton-Century-Crofts, 1965. A description of Freshman Composition in the mid-1960s and recommendations concerning what the course should be. Particularly interesting for teachers interested in knowing about trends in freshman writing courses.

Graves, Richard L., ed. Rhetoric and Composition: A Sourcebook for Teachers. Rochelle Park, N.J.: Hayden, 1976. A collection of thirty-five essays on rhetoric and composition arranged under the headings "Introduction," "Motivating Student Writing," "A Reluctant Medium: The Sentence," "The Paragraph and Beyond," "The Pedagogy of Composition," and "The Uses of Classical Rhetoric."

Kitzhaber, Albert. Themes, Theories, and Therapy: The Teaching of Writing in College. New York: McGraw-Hill, 1963. A critical assessment of the nature of freshman writing courses in the early 1960s, including an explanation of the various "panaceas" for teaching students to be good writers. Extensive recommendations for what college writing courses should be.

Laird, Charlton. The Miracle of Language. Cleveland: World, 1953. Because of its imaginative organization and presentation, this is perhaps the best introduction to the study of language available to a freshman.

Larson, Richard L. "Selected Bibliography of Research and Writing about the Teaching of Composition, 1973-74." *College Composition and Communication*, May 1975. A selective annotated bibliography of articles and books about written composition in 1973 and 1974. The May issue of *College Composition and Communication* for each year since 1975 contains a similar bibliography by Larson of writing about composition. Most of the items included each year were published the year before.

Sentence and the Paragraph, The. Champaign, Ill.: National Council of Teachers of English, 1966. This booklet contains articles that challenge traditional concepts of the nature of the sentence and the paragraph. All of the articles were published in *College Composition and Communication* in the 1960s.

Smith, Ron. "The Composition Requirement Today: A Report on a Nationwide Survey of Four-Year Colleges and Universities." *College Composition and Communication*, May 1974. A comprehensive study of the changes that occurred in the freshman English requirement in the early 1970s. The report is based on information gathered from about 500 schools in 1973. Smith continues his report by discussing the free responses made by respondents to his questionnaire, in "A Further Look into the Fall 1973 Survey," *Freshman English News*, Winter 1975.

Tate, Gary, ed. *Teaching Composition: 10 Bibliographical Essays*. Fort Worth, Tex.: Texas Christian Univ. Press, 1976. Each essayist concentrates on important works written about a particular area in composition. The contents: "Invention: A Topographical Survey," "Structure and Form in Non-Fiction Prose," "Approaches to the Study of Style," "Modes of Discourse," "Basic Writing," "The Uses of Media in Teaching Composition," "Linguistics and Composition," "Rhetorical Analysis of Writing," "Composition and Related Fields," and "Dialects and Composition."

HISTORY OF THE ENGLISH LANGUAGE

Baugh, Albert C. *History of the English Language*. 2nd ed. New York: Appleton-Century-Crofts, 1957. The standard history of the English language.

Francis, W. Nelson. *The History of English*. New York: Norton, 1963. A concise introduction to the development of written and spoken English.

Jespersen, Otto. *The Growth and Structure of the English Language*. New York: Appleton-Century-Crofts, 1923. Also available in paperback published by The Free Press. One of the major histories of the English language.

Pyles, Thomas. *The Origins and Development of the English Language*. New York: Harcourt, Brace, 1964. A good history of the language.

Robertson, Stuart. *The Development of Modern English*, revised by Frederic G. Cassidy. Englewood Cliffs, N.J.: Prentice-Hall, 1954. A survey of the historical backgrounds of modern English.

GRAMMAR

Chomsky, Noam. *Aspects of the Theory of Syntax*. Cambridge, Mass.: M.I.T. Press, 1965. A review and reformulation of the theory of a transformational-generative grammar which Chomsky published in *Syntactic Structures* in 1957. Because of Chomsky's leadership in transformational grammar, this volume may be considered the basic text for the study of the transformational theory. It includes a bibliography which identifies other contributions.

Curme, George O. *Syntax*. Boston: Heath, 1931. A comprehensive, authoritative explanation of the traditional approach to grammar.

Francis, W. Nelson. *The Structure of American English*. New York: Ronald Press, 1958. An analysis of the means by which grammatical distinctions are made in English, with emphasis on sound structures. Written as a textbook for advanced undergraduates and graduates.

Fries, Charles C. *American English Grammar*. New York: Appleton-Century-Crofts, 1940. A description of the grammar of American English based on an analysis of more than 2,000 letters written to a government agency. The result is both a helpful description of educated American language practices and an example of a scientific method applied to a description of grammar.

----------. *The Structure of English*. New York: Harcourt, Brace, 1952. A description of sentence structure based on an analysis of recorded conversations amounting to 250,000 words. Although the analysis has been criticized by other structural grammarians on the grounds that it does not pay sufficient attention to sound, the book is one of the influential documents of structural grammar.

Hunt, Kellogg W. *Grammatical Structures Written at Three Grade Levels*. Champaign, Ill.: National Council of Teachers of English, 1965. This research report has provided the basis for much of the research in sentence maturity done in the past decade. Hunt developed the "T-unit," the most useful instrument now available for studying sentence maturity. The author's extension of his original study is reported in his *Syntactic Maturity in Schoolchildren and Adults* (Chicago: Society for Research in Child Development, 1970) and "Teaching Syntactic Maturity" (in *Applications of Linguistics. Selected papers of the Second International Congress of Applied Linguistics, Cambridge 1969*, ed. G. E. Perren and J. L. M. Trim. Cambridge Univ. Press, 1971). In the last two reports Hunt offers cautious statements about the usefulness of his findings to curriculum makers and teachers of writing.

Long, Ralph B. *The Sentence and Its Parts*. Chicago: Univ. of Chicago Press, 1961. A traditional one-volume grammar of contemporary American English.

Neuleib, Janice. "The Relation of Formal Grammar to Composition." *College Composition and Communication*, October 1977. Reports on four studies that speak of the effect of the teaching of grammar on students' writing abilities: Harris (1962), Bateman-Zidonis (1964), Mellon (1969), and Elley (1976).

insists that the evidence is still not sufficiently conclusive to justify the insistence by Braddock, Lloyd-Jones, and Schoer (1963) that instruction in grammar does not help students improve their writing.

Newkirk, Thomas. "Grammar Instruction and Writing: What We Don't Know." The English Journal, December 1978. Without insisting that grammar should be taught in English classes, the author questions the validity of research that is the basis for the contention that the study of grammar has no positive effect on students' writing ability.

Petrosky, Anthony R. "Grammar Instruction: What We Know." The English Journal, December 1977. Reports that the findings of two "thoroughly designed" research projects (Harris, 1962, and Elley, 1976) indicate that "No empirical evidence exists for the teaching of grammar for any purpose."

Thomas, Owen. "Grammatici Certant." English Journal, May 1963. A brief and elementary discussion of the distinguishing features of traditional, historical, structural, and generative grammar. The author suggests that generative grammar is "a synthesis of the best features of the three earlier grammars."

──────────. Transformational Grammar and the Teacher of English. New York: Holt, Rinehart and Winston, 1965. A simplified account of transformational analysis designed as a textbook to be used by departments of English, schools of education, and secondary school teachers.

USAGE

Bernstein, Theodore M. The Careful Writer: A Modern Guide to English Usage. New York: Atheneum, 1965. This volume represents the conservative position with respect to usage, as Evans (below) represents the liberal position.

Bryant, Margaret M. Current American Usage. New York: Funk & Wagnalls, 1962. This is a scholarly study of usage rather than one based on subjective judgments. It is much less comprehensive than the books by Bernstein, Evans, and Fowler, but on matters on which it reports it may be said to be the standard reference.

Ebbitt, Wilma R., and David R. Ebbitt. Writer's Guide and Index to English. 6th ed. Glenview, Ill.: Scott, Foresman, 1978. Comprehensively applies the results of usage studies to the work in college composition; a revision of the text originally written by Porter C. Perrin.

Eskey, David E. "The Case for the Standard Language." College English, April 1974. Argues that every student should have the opportunity to master Standard English as his or her written language, but that this form should not be forced on the student. Insists that teachers should not suggest that any dialect is inherently inferior or superior to others.

Evans, Bergen, and Cornelia Evans. A Dictionary of Contemporary American Usage. New York: Random House, 1957. More comprehensive and detailed than Bernstein's book. More liberal than the Bernstein volume.

Fowler, H. W. *A Dictionary of Modern English Usage.* 2nd ed.; revised and edited by Sir Ernest Gowers. New York: Oxford Univ. Press, 1965. This revision of an old favorite has been acclaimed as preserving the qualities that made the first edition so popular, while bringing it up to date. The usage is primarily British English.

Freeman, Lawrence D. "The Students' Right to Their Own Language: Its Legal Bases." *College Composition and Communication*, February 1975. The author's purpose is "to describe briefly the substantial legal justification for the resolution on the students' right to their own language." He states that a "state policy of linguistic neutrality" may be legally obligatory and that perhaps the state is legally required to provide teachers who have mastered "the patterns and varieties of language to which the student has become acculturated."

Gorrell, Robert M. "Usage as Rhetoric." *College Composition and Communication*, February 1979. Explains that usage questions are not questions in grammar, but in rhetoric. Whatever concern the writer or speaker has about usage should be about the acceptance of his language by his audience.

Koper, Peter T. "Authority as Emancipator in the Composition Classroom." *Freshman English News*, Winter 1977. A sentence-by-sentence examination of the CCC resolution about "students' right to their own . . . language." Praises the intent of the writers to denounce racism, but argues that the resolution can contribute to students' not learning the dialect that will enable them to exercise freedom of speech in a society that uses what is called Standard English.

Meyers, Walter E. "A Study of Usage Items." *College Composition and Communication*, May 1972. A report on contemporary usage with the data drawn from the Brown University Corpus of American English, a collection of five hundred selections totaling more than one million words. Compares the findings of this study with statements about usage in dictionaries and handbooks.

Perrin, Porter G., and others. *See* Ebbitt, Wilma R., and David R. Ebbitt.

Pixton, William H. "A Contemporary Dilemma: The Question of Standard English." *College Composition and Communication*, October 1974. Written in opposition to the CCC resolution "The Students' Right to Their Own Language." Argues that Standard English does exist, that it is not predicated on racism, and that the student who does not master it is handicapped as an employee.

Pooley, Robert C. "The NCTE and English Usage." *The English Journal*, December 1977. Speaks briefly of the influence of three works--written by Charles Fries, Sterling Leonard, and Robert Pooley in the 1920s and 1930s--on a revolution in the attitudes that texts have expressed toward English usage.

----------. *The Teaching of English Usage.* Urbana, Ill.: National Council of Teachers of English, 1974. A revision of an earlier volume called *Teaching English Usage*. Pooley's work is noted as a calm, carefully reasoned statement on a highly controversial subject.

"Responses to 'The Students' Right to Their Own Language.'" College Composition and Communication, May 1975. In separate responses Ann E. Berthoff and William G. Clark object to the CCC resolution called "The Students' Right to Their Own Language." Berthoff thinks the resolution and its supporting bibliography are the result of "sham scholarship"; she describes the resolution as "cautionary sermonizing" and "sloganeering." Clark thinks the writers of the resolution abandoned their original position (see the beginning of the resolution below) and ended by recommending that Edited American English, which he considers a euphemism for Standard English, be taught to "students who are going into occupations which require formal writing."

"Students' Right to Their Own Language." College Composition and Communication, Fall 1974 (Special Issue). Includes the resolution adopted at the 1974 Conference on College Composition and Communication which begins with "We affirm the students' right to their own patterns and varieties of language--the dialects of their nurture or whatever dialects in which they find their own identity and style." Attempts to answer fifteen questions, a number of them about the nature and effects of dialects. The last of the questions is "What Sort of Knowledge about Language Do English Teachers Need?" Contains an extensive bibliography.

RHETORIC

Becker, A. L. "A Tagmemic Approach to Paragraph Analysis." College Composition and Communication, December 1965. (Also in The Sentence and the Paragraph. Champaign, Ill.: National Council of Teachers of English, 1966.) The author says that his purpose is to show how the tagmemic theory of grammar "can be extended to the description of paragraphs." He discusses two basic paragraph patterns, emphasizing that meaning and form cannot be separated.

Braddock, Richard. "Teaching Rhetorical Analysis." In Rhetoric: Theories for Application, ed. Robert M. Gorrell. Champaign, Ill.: National Council of Teachers of English, 1967. Shows the usefulness of the terms proposition, issues, and evidence in teaching students to write persuasive papers. Also emphasizes the importance of the writer's understanding the position of those who do not agree with the paper's proposition.

Braddock, Richard, Richard Lloyd-Jones, and Lowell Schoer. Research in Written Composition. Champaign, Ill.: National Council of Teachers of English, 1963. A comprehensive statement of what research says about the teaching of writing. In-depth analyses of five valuable research studies.

Burke, Kenneth. A Grammar of Motives and A Rhetoric of Motives. Berkeley: Univ. of California Press, 1969. These two books together present the major development of Burke's treatment of rhetoric. They are available in paperback from the original publisher.

----------. "Questions and Answers about the Pentad." College Composition and Communication, December 1978. Burke explains that one difference between his pentad and Aristotle's Rhetoric is that "the pentad is in effect telling the writer what to ask" about a text already written and that the <u>Rhetoric</u> "is telling the writer what to say." Burke offers an explanation of why his pentad has been adapted for helping writers discover what to say.

Burke, Virginia M. "The Paragraph: Dancer in Chains." In <u>Rhetoric: Theories for Application</u>, ed. Robert M. Gorrell. Champaign, Ill.: National Council of Teachers of English, 1967. Emphasizes that traditional views of the paragraph present it as a "particle" without seeing its "wave" characteristics and its functions in "the total field of meaning."

Christensen, Francis. <u>Notes Toward a New Rhetoric: Six Essays for Teachers</u>. New York: Harper, 1967. A statement of Christensen's popular and influential "generative" analysis of sentences, paragraphs, and larger compositions.

Corbett, Edward P. J. "A New Look at Old Rhetoric." In <u>Rhetoric: Theories for Application</u>, ed. Robert M. Gorrell. Champaign, Ill.: National Council of Teachers of English, 1967. The author recommends those characteristics of classical rhetoric that he thinks are appropriate for contemporary students of composition.

Day-Lewis, C. "The Making of a Poem." <u>Saturday Evening Post</u>, January 21, 1961. A poet's explanation of invention as the search for the theme of a poem and of the similarity between scientific and poetic invention.

Elledge, Scott B. <u>Invention and Topics: or, Where to Look for Something to Say</u>. New York: College Entrance Examination Board, 1965. A kinescript addressed to teachers of English. Presents three kinds of teaching devices intended to help students discover what to say about a subject.

Golden, James L., Goodwin F. Bergquist, and William E. Coleman, eds. <u>The Rhetoric of Western Thought</u>. Dubuque, Iowa: Kendal/Hunt, 1976. Arranged into four parts: "Classical Rhetorical Theory," "British Rhetorical Theory," "Contemporary Rhetoric: Theory and Theorists," "Contemporary Rhetoric: Exploratory Essays." Extensive explanations of the work of major rhetoricians.

Guth, Hans P. "The Politics of Rhetoric." <u>College Composition and Communication</u>, February 1972. An assessment of the strengths and weaknesses of three kinds of rhetoric: conservative, liberal, and radical. A brief recommendation for the writer's capitalizing on the strengths and avoiding the weaknesses of each.

Hairston, Maxine. "Carl Rogers's Alternative to Traditional Rhetoric." <u>College Composition and Communication</u>, December 1976. Explains the advantages and difficulties of teaching students to use Rogers's nonthreatening strategy for persuading people to change their opinions. Offers a five-step plan for using the strategy.

Johannesen, Richard L. "Some Pedagogical Implications of Richard M. Weaver's Views on Rhetoric." <u>College Composition and Communication</u>, October 1978. Draws from a number of Weaver's works to explain the basic tenets of that rhetorician's thinking. Explains Weaver's beliefs about (1) the persuasiveness of all language, (2) the importance of values to the rhetorician, and (3) the nature of argument.

Kinney, James. "Tagmemic Rhetoric: A Reconsideration." College Composition and Communication, May 1978. The author thinks tagmemic theory has little value in helping the writer generate ideas, but that it can be useful when the writer is in the editing stage. (See also Lee Odell, "Another Look at Tagmemic Theory: A Response to James Kinney, College Composition and Communication, May 1978.)

Kneupper, Charles W. "Teaching Argument: An Introduction to the Toulmin Model." College Composition and Communication, October 1978. Simplifies the Toulmin model for argument. Explains how Toulmin's work can be useful in teaching argument, particularly how it can help students write logically sound outlines.

Koestler, Arthur. The Act of Creation. New York: Macmillan, 1964. Also available in paperback. A comprehensive and readable analysis of the process of invention in art and science.

Lunsford, Andrea A. "Aristotelian vs. Rogerian Argument: A Reassessment." College Composition and Communication, May 1979. Argues that Aristotelian and Rogerian principles of persuasion are much more similar than current scholars in rhetoric have acknowledged. Emphasizes Aristotle's concern that the speaker should establish identification with the audience.

Odell, Lee. "Piaget, Problem-Solving, and Freshman Composition." College Composition and Communication, February 1973. Describes a system that helps composition students formulate a problem competently and then discover how to resolve the problem. Advocates Kenneth Pike's method of analyzing through tagmemics.

Rapoport, Anatol. "Ethical Debate." In Fights, Games, and Debates. Ann Arbor: Univ. Michigan Press, 1960. The first two parts of this book require a considerable background in mathematics, but Part III requires no such preparation and is valuable as a modern approach to persuasion.

Rohman, D. Gordon. "Pre-Writing: The Stage of Discovery in the Writing Process." College Composition and Communication, May 1965. The article is a digest of a report for Project English by Rohman and associates ("Construction and Application of Models for Concept Formation in Writing," U.S. Office of Education Cooperative Research Project No. 2174). The full report is available in libraries. The researchers conclude that prewriting activities that they tested can contribute to the quality of students' writing.

Toulmin, Stephen. The Uses of Argument. Cambridge: Cambridge Univ. Press, 1969. A collection of five essays, with an introduction and a conclusion, intended to stir debate on the nature of deductive reasoning. Toulmin is concerned with how usable conclusions can be discovered through argument. He insists that syllogistic reasoning is often too simplistic to lead to accurate conclusions and that useful ways of arguing in one field may not be appropriate for another field.

Winterowd, W. Ross, ed. Contemporary Rhetoric: A Conceptual Background with Readings. New York: Harcourt Brace Jovanovich, 1975. Winterowd's extensive introduction on pedagogy is followed by twenty-four essays, including several of the best-known essays by contemporary teacher-rhetoricians. They are arranged under the headings "Invention," "Form," and "Style."

Young, Richard E., Alton L. Becker, and Kenneth Pike. Rhetoric: Discovery and Change. New York: Harcourt, Brace, 1970. This book develops into a composition text the basic concepts of trimodal analysis. Whereas other linguists have chiefly been concerned with the rhetoric of sentences and paragraphs, this book is a systematic rhetoric which applies field theory to the problems of invention, arrangement, and style.

SEMANTICS

Brown, Roger. Words and Things. New York: The Free Press, 1958. A readable synthesis of much of the scholarship in anthropology, linguistics, philosophy, and psychology having to do with the relation of words and things.

Burke, Kenneth. "Definition of Man." In Language as Symbolic Action. Berkeley: Univ. of California Press, 1968. The clearest introduction to Burke's thesis that language is man's second nature and the source of powerful drives which make him the "symbol-using animal."

Hayakawa, S. I., with others. Language in Thought and Action. 4th ed. New York: Harcourt Brace Jovanovich, 1978. A fourth revision of an earlier edition, entitled Language in Action, a popularization of Alfred Korzybski's Science and Sanity, and probably the most widely read book on semantics.

Hayakawa, S. I., ed. Language, Meaning and Maturity: Selections from ETC: A Review of General Semantics, 1943-1953. New York: Harper, 1954. A collection of essays in semantics and widely separated fields, all centering on the problems of language and symbolism.

Lee, Irving J. Language Habits in Human Affairs. New York: Harper, 1941. Another popularization of Korzybski's work, unusually rich in illustrative material.

Ogden, C. K., and I. A. Richards. The Meaning of Meaning. 3rd ed. New York: Harcourt, Brace, 1930. Also available in paperback as a Harvest Book. One of the earliest and most influential of the works on semantics.

Thurman, Kelly, ed. Semantics. Boston: Houghton Mifflin, 1960. Contains many excerpts from the works of semanticists; organized into three sections: "Basic Principles," "Semantics at Work," and "Criticisms of Semantics." Suitable for the reader who wants to get an overview of semantics quickly.

Whorf, Benjamin Lee. Language, Thought, and Reality. Cambridge, Mass.: M.I.T. Press, 1956. A collection of Whorf's writings emphasizing language as a means of perceiving and interpreting reality.

STYLE

Beardsley, Monroe L. "Style and Good Style." In Reflections on High School English: NDEA Institute Lectures 1965, ed. Gary Tate. Tulsa: Univ. of Tulsa Press, 1966. Views style and meaning as inseparable and insists that any change in style creates a corresponding change in meaning. The article is largely concerned with the implications of this view for the teacher of composition.

Braddock, Richard. "The Frequency and Placement of Topic Sentences in Expository Prose." *Research in the Teaching of English*, Winter 1974. This study of topic sentences in twenty-five essays written by professional writers shows that most paragraphs in this body of material neither begin nor end with topic sentences. But the writer does not argue that teachers of composition should cease encouraging students to build paragraphs around topic sentences.

D'Angelo, Frank J. "Imitation and Style." *College Composition and Communication*, October 1973. Shows how imitation of an author's style can bring variety to a student's writing. The demonstration is based on an excerpt from Irwin Shaw's "The Eighty-Yard Run."

Gibson, Walker. *The "Speaking Voice" and the Teaching of Composition*. New York: College Entrance Examination Board, 1965. A kinescript addressed to teachers of English. Discusses the role of the "speaking voice" in written composition. Helpful illustrative material.

Mellon, John C. *Transformational Sentence-Combining: A Method for Enhancing the Development of Syntactic Fluency in English Composition*. Urbana, Ill.: National Council of Teachers of English, 1969. A report on a successful experiment intended to heighten "the growth rate of children's syntactic fluency."

Memering, Dean. "Forward to the Basics." *College English*, January 1978. Insists that composition teachers cannot avoid the demand that they should teach sentence level skills and suggests that sentence-combining instruction (as developed by O'Hare, without attention to grammar) offers the best hope of success. This instruction need not replace but should supplement other approaches to teaching composition.

Morenburg, Max, Donald Daiker, and Andrew Kerek. "Sentence Combining at the College Level: An Experimental Study." *Research in the Teaching of English*, October 1978. The researchers report that college freshmen whose composition course consisted primarily of sentence-combining work scored "significantly higher than a reference group" on scales measuring "syntactic maturity" and "overall writing quality." (A less detailed report on the study appears in *College Composition and Communication*, February 1978.)

Morse, J. Mitchell. "Why Write Like a College Graduate?" *College English*, October 1970. A rejection of "the snob appeal of the so called 'correct' forms" of English and an argument for teachers' trying to arouse in their students "an emotional concern for clarity and precision" in language.

O'Hare, Frank. *Sentence Combining: Improving Student Writing without Formal Grammar Instruction*. Urbana, Ill.: National Council of Teachers of English, 1973. A research report that concludes that training in sentence-combining exercises can enhance the syntactical maturity of seventh grade students' writing and that this maturity contributes to the quality of the essays they write.

Rogers, Paul C., Jr. "A Discourse-centered Rhetoric of the Paragraph." College Composition and Communication, February 1966. (Also in The Sentence and the Paragraph. Champaign, Ill.: National Council of Teachers of English, 1966.) Suggests that traditional deductive reasoning about the nature of the paragraph must yield to description developed through inductive analysis. Emphasizes "the general flow of discourse" rather than individual paragraph units.

Strunk, William S., Jr., and E. B. White. Elements of Style. New York: Macmillan, 1959. A brief and elementary work that teachers often recommend to students for individual study. The original handbook of "do's" and "don't's," by Professor Strunk, was revised in minor ways by White. The final chapter, on style, is White's.

TEACHING

Brown, Dorothy S. "The Perils of Plagiarism." College Composition and Communication, May 1975. Largely a transcript of a tape on which students discuss their frustrations over their failure to understand what constitutes plagiarism in research papers.

Christensen, Francis. "The Course in Advanced Composition for Teachers." College Composition and Communication, May 1973. The author identifies and discusses, among other matters, elements of composition in which the teacher of writing should be competent.

D'Angelo, Frank J. "The Search for Intelligible Structure in the Teaching of Composition." College Composition and Communication, May 1976. Insists that "composition does have an underlying structure which gives unity and coherence to the field." Distinguishes between principles and forms of discourse and discusses briefly four modern forms: expressive, persuasive, referential, and literary. Concludes with a discussion of what may be achieved through a discovery of the underlying structure of the composition discipline.

Diederich, Paul B. Measuring Growth in English. Urbana, Ill.: National Council of Teachers of English, 1974. A new publication in which Diederich assimilates what he has learned over the years about measurement of writing. Two chapters, "Factors in Judgments of Writing Ability" and "The Effect of Bias," are particularly important for the teacher of composition.

Fenstermaker, John J. "Literature in the Composition Class." College Composition and Communication, February 1977. Argues for the value of literature in the last course of the freshman composition sequence but insists that the course must not be primarily one in literary criticism. Writing assignments should be on subjects and themes that are important to students, and the instructor should capitalize on the study of patterns of organization in earlier courses.

Freedom and Discipline in English: Report of the Commission on English. New York: College Entrance Examination Board, 1965. Contains a chapter on the teaching of composition, with sections on organizing the instruction, making assignments, and evaluating writing.

Gorrell, Robert M. "The Traditional Course: When Is Old Hat New?" College Composition and Communication. October 1972. Argues that the composition course should be organized around the academic discipline of rhetoric and that such a course "is not incompatible with devotion to the development of the student."

Guth, Hans P. English Today and Tomorrow. Englewood Cliffs, N.J.: Prentice-Hall, 1964. A survey of English as a school subject and of the teaching of English as a profession. Although written as a guide for teachers and those who intend to become teachers of English, it is of general interest.

Haynes, Elizabeth F. "Using Research in Preparing to Teach Writing." The English Journal, January 1978. A closely documented essay about what research says about the effectiveness of "eight means used to improve composition . . . --traditional grammar, structural linguistics, transformational grammar, sentence-combining practice, frequency of writing, intensive correction, increased reading, and precomposition experiences."

Kehl, D. G. "The Electric Carrot: The Rhetoric of Advertisement." College Composition and Communication, May 1975. The author presents a number of examples to support his belief that through the study of advertisements "the students can learn about virtually every composition/rhetorical strategy."

Larson, Richard L. "Discovery Through Questioning: A Plan for Teaching Rhetorical Invention." College English, November 1968. Argues that students can discover what is worth saying about their subjects through responding to carefully worded questions. Suggests that this discovery may cause them to have respect for their writing.

McNamara, John. "Teaching the Process of Writing." College English, February 1973. Emphasizes the influence of audience on the discourse. Stresses cooperative writing tasks in which both the students and the instructor are participants.

Moffett, James. Teaching the Universe of Discourse. Boston: Houghton Mifflin, 1968. Though chiefly concerned with teaching English at precollege levels, the material on the interrelation of grammar, literature, and composition, and that on teaching procedures, can be helpful to college instructors.

Snipes, Wilson Currin. "Oral Composing as an Approach to Writing." College Composition and Communication, May 1973. Description of a method that teaches students to develop papers through a "talking-retalking-writing-rewriting" sequence.

"What's Working Well for Us." Freshman English News, Winter 1974. A group of short statements by directors of freshman composition programs. The statements were in response to the editor's invitation to describe in 300-400 words the most successful features of the programs at their schools.

In order to meet the changing needs of instructors and students in future editions of <u>Writing with a Purpose</u>, we would like to receive your evaluation of the present edition. The text is designed for a two-semester course, and we ask that you complete the following questionnaire after you have used <u>Writing with a Purpose</u> for one full year. Please mail your comments to

> James M. McCrimmon
> c/o Marketing Services
> College Division
> Houghton Mifflin Company
> One Beacon Street
> Boston, Massachusetts 02107

1. Which chapters did you assign? (Please circle.)

    1   2   3   4   5   6   7   8   9   10   11   12   13   14

2. Which of the assigned chapters did you find most helpful?

    1   2   3   4   5   6   7   8   9   10   11   12   13   14

3. Which chapters did you find least helpful?

    1   2   3   4   5   6   7   8   9   10   11   12   13   14

4. What major revisions of the chapters circled in question 3 would make the book more helpful to your students?

5. Are any major topics omitted that should be treated either in an existing chapter or in a separate chapter?

6. Is the style of the book generally appropriate for your students?

7. Is the "Handbook" section adequate for your students' needs? If not, how can it be improved?

8. Have you found the instructor's manual helpful? What changes or additions would you like to see made?

9. Please add any further comments about <u>Writing with a Purpose</u> that should be considered in future editions. (Continue on an additional sheet if necessary.)